AMSTERDAM
ART GUIDE

Christian Reinewald

Art Guide Publications

Also available in this series:

LONDON ART AND ARTISTS GUIDE
ISBN 0 9507160 7 3

PARIS ART GUIDE
ISBN 0 9507160 6 5

NEW YORK ART GUIDE
ISBN 0 9507160 9 X

AUSTRALIAN ARTS GUIDE
ISBN 0 9507160 8 1

BERLIN ARTS GUIDE
ISBN 0 946716 40 4

THE ARTISTS DIRECTORY
ISBN 0 9 46716 00 5

AMSTERDAM ART GUIDE
Christian Reinewald
ISBN 0 946716 35 8
First Edition 1985

This publication is protected by international copyright law. All rights reserved. No part of this publication may be reproduced, stored in a retrieval system or transmitted in any form or by any means electronic, mechanical, photocopying or otherwise without the prior permission of the publishers.

Whilst every care has been taken to ensure accuracy throughout this book, the publishers cannot accept responsibility for any errors which may appear.

Photographs copyright Christian Reinewald © 1985
Text copyright Christian Reinewald © 1985
Maps copyright A. W. Peetoom © 1985

ISBN O 946716 35 8
British Library Cataloguing in Publication Data
Reinewald Christian
Amsterdam Art Guide — 1st ed. — (Art Guide series)
Amsterdam (Netherlands) — Description Guide Books
Title 914.92'3 DJ411.A53
Published by Art Guide Publications
28 Colville Road London W11 2BS Tel 01-299 4669

Printed in Great Britain by
Archway Press Limited Poole Dorset England

ART GUIDE PUBLICATIONS

2nd edition 1985

The Artists Directory

Richard Layzell
Heather Waddell

The Artist's Directory is a comprehensive art handbook for artists, art world people, arts administrators, Arts Councils and the interested art public. It covers advice for artists about exhibiting, useful art addresses, gallery information throughout Britain (divided regionally), art supply shops, bookshops, magazines, art schools, awards, competitions and studios. It also has sections on tax and artlaw, sponsorship, art in public places, the role of the British Council and Arts Councils, an international section for art travellers and a useful art bibliography.

The Artist's Directory is aimed at the contemporary art world and is essential reading matter for everyone involved in the contemporary art world in Britain. The main emphasis is to provide artists with useful and essential information but the book will also prove invaluable for its extensive listings of contemporary art galleries and art information throughout Britain.

ISBN 0 9467160 05   £6.95 $14.00

200 pages 30 b/w photographs 2nd edition

Paris Art Guide
London Art and Artists Guide
Australian Arts Guide
New York Art Guide
Art Diary
Flash Art International magazine
The Artists Directory

The **Paris Art Guide** (2nd edition), a new, enlarged, revised edition contains details of art galleries, museums, print studios, art and photography classes, art suppliers, bookshops, art organisations, summer festivals as well as restaurants, café-theatres, music places, parks and markets and general information on Paris. 128pp, 14 photographs, 2 art maps. A French edition will be published by Librairie Grund, Paris, in 1983.

The **London Art and Artists Guide** (3rd edition) is a comprehensive pocket art guide to London. The guide covers 500 galleries divided into five sections: museums, galleries dealing in 1900 art, contemporary art galleries, national centres and institutes and alternative art spaces. Useful art addresses, studios, workshops, evening classes, art supply shops, artists groups, art magazines and art bookshops are also included. The London information covers transport, restaurants area by area, pubs, tea places, parks, markets, music places and sport. There are 25 b/w photographs, 4 maps.

The **Australian Arts Guide** covers galleries, theatres, music venues and other arts information in all the major Australian cities. It also covers restaurants, travel within Australia, useful information and addresses, making it a useful guide for both Australians and visitors to Australia. 10 b/w photographs and maps.

The **New York Art Guide** contains similar information to the London guide but relating directly to New York (Manhattan), the world's contemporary art capital, covering galleries Uptown, Midtown, and Downtown. Other information covers restaurants, travel, transport, and useful information for visitors. 16 b/w photographs and maps.

All the pocket art guides are written by someone well acquainted with the city or country, giving them added personal appeal. Wherever possible information about gallery applications has been included to help artists. Details of how to reach the galleries are also indicated in each guide.

Art Diary is published by Flash Art magazine in Milan, Italy and Art Guide Publications will act as UK distributor for both Art Diary and **Flash Art International magazine**. Art Diary covers 38 countries listing professional artists, art critics, galleries and cheap hotels and restaurants. Flash Art International magazine is published quarterly and covers art exhibitions in UK, Europe, the USA and Australia with colour photographs.

Paris Art Guide Editor Fiona Dunlop	Price £3.50	$6.95
ISBN 0 9507160 65, 128 pages 14 b/w photos		
London Art and Artists Guide Editor Heather Waddell Price £3.95		$6.95
ISBN 0 9507160 73, 132 pages 25 b/w photos		
Australian Arts Guide Editor Roslyn Kean	Price £2.50	$5.95
ISBN 0 9501760 3 0, 96 pages 10 b/w photos		
New York Art Guide Editor Deborah Gardner	Price £2.95	$5.95
ISBN 0 9507160 4 9, 128 pages 16 b/w photos		
Art Diary Publisher Flash Art Milan, Italy	Price £12.00	
Flash Art International magazine	Price £2.50 per issue	
Published five times a year	Price £15 p.a. sub	
The Artists Directory 160 pages 12 b/w photos, ISBN 0 9507160 57 (a handbook to the contemporary British Art World) Price £5.95 $12.00		
UK Bookshops should order direct from Ken Dickson Marketing Ltd. Telephone 0990 25421.		

ORDER FORM To: The Address below. Please send me

.........copies of **London Art and Artists Guide**   £3.95 + 50p postage $6.95 + $3.00
.........copies of **Paris Art Guide**   £3.50 + 50p postage $6.95 + $3.00
.........copies of **Australian Art Guide**   £3.95 + 50p postage $5.95 + $3.00
.........copies of **New York Art Guide**   £5.95 + 50p postage $5.95 + $3.00
.........copies of **Art Diary**   £11.00 + 50p postage $20.00 + $3.00
.........copies of **Flash Art International**   annual sub £15.00
.........copies of **The Artist Directory**   £6.95 + 50p postage $12.00 + $3.00
.........copies of **Toronto Art and Artists Guide**   £3.95 + 30p postage $6.95 + $3.00
.........copies of **Amsterdam Arts Guide**   £5.95
.........copies of **Berlin Arts Guide**   £5.95

Name ....

Address ....

Signature... Date............................85/86

Cheques should be made payable to Art Guide Publications and sent to the address below. Once the cheque is received books will be sent by return of post.

ART GUIDE PUBLICATIONS, 28 COLVILLE ROAD, LONDON
W11 2BS   01-229 4669

HOLLAND Nilsson & Lamm, Pampuslaan 212, 1380 Ad Weesp
USA Robert Silver Assoc., 307 East 37th Street, NY 10016
AUSTRALIA Bookwise, PO Box 296, Welland, South Australia 5007

It began with Oblomov
The rest followed
Come and see why!

OPEN DAILY 12 pm-1 am
for lunch and dinner

Tel 020 241074
REGULIERSDWARSSTRAAT 40 AMSTERDAM

WILDSCHUT — Roelof Hartplein 1-3
Tel: 020 768220
DAILY 9.00-3.00

The two most popular Deco style
art pubs in Amsterdam.
Good food at moderate prices.

CAFE SCHILLER — Rembrandtsplein 26
Tel: 020 249846
DAILY 4.00-2.00

CONTENTS

Introduction by Michael Shepherd	7-8
Foreword in Dutch by Christian Reinewald	8-9
Amsterdam in the open air	10
Amsterdam in the rain	13
Museums	13
Museums, museum-area	14
Museums, Jordaan-area	18
Museums outside the centre	21
Museums elsewhere in Holland	23
Antique and art dealers, museum-area	27
Antique and art dealers around Dam/Rokin	30
Antique and art dealers Jordaan-area	31
Auction-houses	31
Commercial galleries	32
Galleries museum-area	33
Galleries Jordaan-area	38
Galleries in other parts of Amsterdam	45
Art hire	46
Art groups and their exhibition spaces	47
Foreign cultural centres	51
Places of architectural interest	53
Printshops print publishers	58
Artists workshops	59
Useful art addresses-artists unions	60
Exhibition-unions	61
Studios	62
Other useful art addresses	63
State aid and subsidies	64
Private subsidies, grants, art prizes	65
Artists materials, fine arts	65
Book-print, print-making	66
Photography, professional labs, equipment	67
Camera-repair etc	68
Copiers	68
Audio-visual, sculpture	69
Framing, displays, show-cases	70
Restoring of prints, paintings	71
Graphic design materials ceramics	71
Fabrics, art-transport, transport van rent	71-72
Insurance	72
Art magazines	73
Newspaper sections, art critics	75
Opinion-weeklies etc	76
Radio-TV	77
Art bookshops/well selected art book section bookshops	78
other interesting bookshops	80
Art posters	82
Art libraries	82
Art schools	82
Private art classes/other art schools	84-85
General information	85
Accommodation	86
Travel in Amsterdam	87
Taxi, bike-hire	87-88

Travel outside Amsterdam, car hire	88
Trains, railway stations	89
Airport, travel abroad	89
Hitch hiking/consulates	90
Cultural reduction passes/bank opening hours	91-92
Shopping hours	92
Police/fire	92
Post Office	93
Parks/botanical gardens	93
Markets	95
Food buying	97
Tea-lunchrooms museum-area	98
Tea-lunchrooms Jordaan-area	99
Cafés around Spui/Spuistraat	101
Cafés around Rembrandts plein	101
Cafés in Jordaan-area/gay bars	102
Theatre-café's/restaurants	103
Restaurants	104
Restaurants museum-area	105
Restaurants around Dam Square	105
Restaurants in Jordaan	109
Restaurants in other locations	110
Night-restaurants	111
Festivals	111
Theatres	112
Cinema's/film-houses	113
Music places	113
Jazz-pop-rock	114
Folk-discos	115
Recreation/sports	116

Innersleeve (left) art map museum-area
Innersleeve (right) art map Jordaan-area

PHOTOGRAPHS
Cover photo: Alexander Schabracq's sculpture with bikes, 1978 4 × 5 metres. On view until recently near the Recht Boomssloot 26 (since April '85 owned by Liesbeth Lips gallery) next to Gallery Sponz

Amstel River	2
Street Magician performing at the Leidesplein gallery	3
Artotheek art hire centre "De Meervaart" Osdorpplein	4
Terrace of the Vincent Van Gogh Museum	5
New wing at the Stedelijk Museum	6
17th Century garden of the Museum Willet Holthuysen on the Amstelstraat	7
Interior Burgerzaal of the Palace Dam Square	8
Old Print Shop, Spiegelgracht	9
Medical antiquities and Dr. Sloane himself on Prinsengracht	10
Exhibition before auction at Sothebys	11
Staircase in Hans Gieles gallery, Spuistraat	12
Jules Farber of Barbara Farber gallery, Herengracht	13
Hans Gieles during Peter Verhaar's exhibition	14
Glassworks in gallery Nanky de Vreeze, Singel	15
Interior of SBK art hire centre, NZ Voorburgwaal	16
Aorta studio and exhibition space, Spuistraat	17

De Schottenburch's Wim Vonk with visitors at his gallery	18
Public library at the British Council Herengracht	19
French Cultural Centre Maison Descartes Vijzelgracht	20
Inside the Rietveld cupola, Metz building (1933) Leidsestraat	21
Cascade building overlooking the Zuiderkersplein	22
Workshop of lithographer Marcel Kalksma of Polychrome, Frans Halsstraat	23
Painter's studio	24
Lithographic materials; gum arabic, sponge and Japanese brush	25
Wool shop "Naturel" in Gasthuismolensteeg	26
Art books at Art Book bookshop on Prinsengracht	27
Art bookshop Robert Premsela opposite the Stedelijk, Van Baerlestraat	28
Open air casting, Rietveld Academie, Fred Roeskestraat	29
Rijksacademie, Stadhouderskade	30
Pole object by Fred van der Linde Amstelpark	31
Fish on sale at Albert Cuyp market	32
Curiosities at the fleamarket Waterlooplein	33
Art deco interior of Café restaurant Americain Leidseplein	34
The Danspaleis temporarily placed during hot summer nights near the Museumstraat	35
Christian Reinewald — the author	36

INTRODUCTION

Amsterdam is one of the most open and welcoming cities in the world. And yet it is also one of the most private. This is due, not to any attitude of its current inhabitants, but rather, its plan and its architectural inheritance. Its semi-circular layout, punctuated by four all-too-similar canals in concentric arcs, makes it, like Venice, a marvellous place to get lost in; but maddeningly difficult for a stranger trying to arrive by a fixed time at a particular address which looks, on the map, just a short brisk walk away. One mistake, and you're like those first sea explorers who thought from the map that the earth was a flat place with straight lines of travel from A to B, but discovered that it was curved; so is it quicker that I'm now at C, or not?

Many's the time I've wished that the Amsterdam art dealers had clubbed together to hand out a free, comradely map showing where they all were. For me, this guide is worth its money for the maps alone.

And this points to another reason why art visitors need a guide to Amsterdam's art scene in all its richness. Whereas in London, for instance, many of the most exciting exhibitions take place in commercial art galleries, the Dutch rightly consider art a matter of prime public concern, and so the most visible face of art tends to be that in the public museums and galleries and art centres. Correspondingly, with Amsterdam's commercial art galleries dotted all around the city — and often keeping very independent hours, if not days — Amsterdam's contemporary art trade is hard to focus on, and get around. I'm a regular professional visitor to Amsterdam's art scene, but this guide is still a revelation to me.

And I think that even Dutch readers (whom Chris Reinewald addresses in Dutch on page 9), particularly those from out-of-town, will be surprised at the score of — for instance — alternative artists' spaces which he has listed; the score of art magazines; and the score of restaurants and bars which they may not yet have tried; as well as, of course, the lists of addresses aimed at working artists. Guides like this, a writer who lives and works in the city, may give away a few local secrets, but they certainly 'know their onions', or do I mean tulip bulbs.

The only thing a local writer can't do is to communicate the sheer visual delights of a stranger to the scene. When Britain is cold, grey, and rainy, when the clouds are heavy, dark, and low, it's just marvellous to take off, by air or by that super Olau ferry like a floating hotel, for a country where the light is clear, the skies wide, the colours strong, the trains clean and warm and on time, meals and clothes well-made and enjoyed, and every detail of the landscape and urban environment thought about, designed, and 'looked at'.

But what is special about Amsterdam's art scene? The Rijksmuseum's evocation of Holland's 'Golden Age'; the art and architecture of the De Stijl group; the Van Gogh Museum; Mondrian's paintings in the Stedelijk; all these of course, but what of the present? Every country has its 'high times', and it can't be said at the moment that Holland leads the world in its art, its architecture, or its museums and galleries. What makes Amsterdam's art scene individual is just what makes any art city individual: the particular mix of national, European, and international tastes and influences, reflected in the national and the individual character. Dutch art means more when seen in the Netherlands; and foreign art can be seen freshly in a new context.

Look at the landscape and the faces, and the Dutch masters are alive in front of you; snoop into the lighted windows of the houses at dusk and you see a perfectly lit still life in every room; look at Dutch design in the shops and you understand the pleasures of the 'modern movement'. A walk round the museums and galleries in the company of visiting Nederlanders, and you catch glimpses of different sorts of Dutch satisfactions. (I think that the Dutch have the secret of seeing any action through to final satisfaction, which other nations could learn from.) And on a fine day in any season, a trip out to the Kröller-Müller museum outside Arnhem teaches one about that other Dutch visual genius — of harmonising nature, architecture both exterior and interior, art, and human beings — in its superb glass-walled galleries, and its great sculpture garden. It makes you feel that you are in a place where art *matters,* and eyes are for looking. And — not to anatomize Dr. Tulp too far — yes, flowers do seem to matter more, in Holland . . .

Well, that's just a little romantic bouquet from the visitor to the host, in the Dutch fashion; to go with this very professional, very useful art guide by a young expert, to that none-too-public art centre, Amsterdam; which artists and visitors from other countries ought to know more about, so that they can enjoy it more fully.

Michael Shepherd

VOORWOORD

Als Amsterdams kunstenaar of kunstliefhebber kun je genoeg kapsones hebben om in de stemmen met de wervende leus "Amsterdam heeft 't". Voor de niet-Amsterdammer blijft echter de vraag waar "'t" dan wel te vinden is in de stad.

Deze Amsterdam Art Guide hoopt hierop vele antwoorden te kunnen geven. Dat de gids in het Engels geschreven is, mag voor de toch veelal internationaal geöriënteerde Nederlandse liefhebber amper een bezwaar zijn.

In de gekozen opzet is namelijk voor het eerst informatie aangedragen en samengebracht over musea, galeries, kunstenaars-initiatieven en -benodigdheden, werkplaatsen, en (kunst)boekhandels, maar ook over restaurants, café's en theaters. Op deze manier kunnen zowel de 'vierdagstoerist' als de hier tijdelijk werkende kunstenaar-eventueel al voor het vertrek-hun voorkeuren opspeuren en aanstrepen.

Wie — zoals ik — de eerder verschenen gidsen van Londen en Parijs (ze zijn er inmiddels ook van New York en Berlijn) heeft gebruikt weet hoe handig ze zijn. Ze komen zeer van pas, en dat niet in de laatste plaats vanwege de plattegronden en de talloze tips, die barre zoektochten naar verscholen galeries of voordelige eetgelegenheden tot een minimum helpen beperken.

Vergeleken met deze Europese hoofdsteden kan Amsterdam niet geuren met al te drukbezochte overzichtstentoonstellingen van grote meesters uit de kunstgeschiedenis. Gelukkig maar, zou je haast zeggen. Onze groten: Rembrandt, Van Gogh en Mondriaan laten zich ieder in een eigen museum rustig bekijken. Daar komt nog bij dat de musea dicht bij elkaar rond het Museumplein gelegen zijn, waar zich ook een groot aantal galeries bevinden.

Amsterdam kenmerkt zich vooral door het grote aanbod van uiteenlopende musea en galeries, waar vrijwel alle ontwikkelingen van de (inter)nationale beeldende en toegepaste kunst te bewonderen zijn.

De relatief lage leeftijd van de meeste galeries zorgt daarbij voor een grote flexibiliteit ten aanzien van nieuwe stijlen en werkwijzen.

Daarnaast bewerkstelligen de verschillende enthousiaste kunstenaarsinitiatieven dat de tentoonstellingsruimten in de stad niet snel in ongenaakbare kunsttempels zullen veranderen.

Al deze elementen vormen bij elkaar sinds oudsher het karakter van de beeldende kunst in Nederland, met eigenzinnigheid en kwaliteit als voornaamste eigenschappen.

Tevens draagt het beleid van de Gemeente Amsterdam bij tot een goed artistiek en kultureel klimaat, waarin het prettig vertoeven is.

Des te droeviger is het dat er juist nu door de regering in Den Haag zo onwijs met kunst en kultuur wordt omgesprongen.

Afsluitend wil ik de mensen bedanken, die mij hebben geholpen bij het maken van de gids:

Robert Alkemade, Fransje Appelman (Naturel), firma Van Beek, Ch A. Boorman, Marcel Kalksma (Polychrome), William Lindhout, Saskia Osterholt (Art Book), Sonja Oudendijk (Aorta), Lex Schabracq, Gerard Spaan, Mevr. M. Tuininga-Meyerink (Ver. van Handelaren in Oude Kunst in Nederland), Wim Vonk (De Schottenburch), Cor Wijtman en de Amsterdamse galeristen, met name Paul Derrez (Ra), Tom van Dijk (Petit), Hans Gieles, Gerard Lageman en Jules Farber (Barbara Farber). Uiteraard dank ik de adverteerders voor hun vertrouwen in de gids.

Zeer veel dank gaat uit naar Lida Peetoom voor haar hulp bij teksten, foto's, kaartjes en advertentieverkoop.

Also I would like to thank Carol Dameron in Amsterdam and Heather Waddell and Michael Shepherd in London for their support, advice and ideas.

Christian Reinewald, februari 1985

AMSTERDAM IN THE OPEN AIR

Like every modern capital Amsterdam possesses charms like wandering around shopping-centres: just looking, going in and out of the fashion-shops around Kalverstraat and Nieuwendijk, or buying second-hand clothing in the Jordaan. Especially the Leidsestraat, which with travel-agencies, book- and record shops and nearby art galleries has its own Saturday-flâneurs.

Finding your way along the canals can be rather confusing. Remember all canals and most streets are odd/even numbered from the centre: Central Station outwards; low numbers near Central Station, high numbers near the river Amstel. The sequence of the canals outwards from Dam-square is Singel, Herengracht, Keizersgracht and Prinsengracht.

Canals have no tram, bus or metro-stops, so you must walk from the streets or squares nearby.

Starting with the April 30th birthday of the former Queen Juliana and now established as a festival day, off-street activities take place. Professional theatre-groups perform and amateur-musicians play their musical exercises in front of a live audience.

Also a special "vrij-markt" (free-market) is held every Queensday, when everyone is allowed to perform or to sell things.

Later, in June, when cultural festivals such as the "Holland Festival" and its alternative "Festival of Fools" take place, the city becomes crowded with foreign acrobats, clowns, musicians and street-theatre groups. The busiest area is around the Leidseplein in front of the Stadsschouwburg (Municipal Theatre), in the subway of the Rijksmuseum or somewhere in the Vondelpark, near the Leidseplein.

Another park, which can really compare with the Bois de Boulogne in Paris is the Amsterdamse Bos, south of the city near Amstelveen. (see: parks and botanical gardens).

If you are looking for picturesque small Dutch wooden houses you have to head north of Amsterdam, where the city-governed villages Holysloot, Ransdorp and Durgerdam still overlook green fields. Without doubt you'll find the flattest landscape you ever dreamt of. Your eyes travel to infinity across the skies, across green fields and straight ditches, sprinkled with colour. Some say that you'll find clues to Dutch art, figurative and abstract, here.

Down south following the Amstel-river to more scenic villages, Ouderkerk and Abcoude provide another nice alternative way to spend a lazy afternoon in summer. The best way to do all this is to hire a bike.

Whether it's cloudy or clear in Amsterdam, some will like to replace the traditional boat-trip through the canals by an expedition on foot; especially on Sunday, when there is less traffic, you'll enjoy walking in the canal-zone, imagining you lived in bygone days.

Some quarters of Amsterdam reflect the past up until today. The Prinseneiland, located north-west of the Central Station next to the Haarlemmer Houttuinen (Haarlem Timber yards) has not only the name but also the flavour of the old days, when wooden ships were repaired here, because nowadays house-boats are still lying on the slipways.

The Jordaan-quarter, which is named after the French 'jardin', garden, is the place where the proud and popular Jordanese people live. Most of them are lineal descendants of the French labourers, who were hired by the municipality to construct the canals. The names of the

Amstel River

streets in the Jordaan refer to flowers or plants. Today young entrepreneurs have transformed some streets into shopping-areas with cafés and fashion-stores. Once a year, during the Jordaan Festival, the traditional Jordanese inhabitants return to sing and dance the popular tunes, together with the new Jordanese; artists and students.

Slightly exotic and erotic is the Nieuwmarkt-quarter, east of Central Station and Dam-square. The streets behind the impressive St Nicolas Church (Nicolas protects Amsterdam just like the Russian city of Leningrad) are crowded with people, dealing in drugs of doubtful quality. Somewhere near the Nieuwmarkt and Binnen Bantammerstraat, Amsterdam's tiny China Town is located.

Around the Oudekerksplein and Oude Zijds Achterburgwal is the red light district.

Near the Amstel river you'll find Amsterdam's flea-market, the Waterlooplein. (see: Markets).

Places of architectural interest are spread out all over Amsterdam. As well as the typical canal-houses, containing the more exclusive art galleries, the "Amsterdam School" building blocks are worth a visit. (see: Architectural interest).

Never leave Amsterdam without spending some time in the Begijnhof, the Beguinage, which serves as an oasis in the hectic life of the city. Here you can find also Amsterdam's oldest wooden house, as well as Ye Olde English Church.

Street magician performing his tricks, Leidseplein

AMSTERDAM IN THE RAIN

Some say Amsterdam is at its best when autumn rains fall. On rainy days one tends to escape to the big stores like Vroom & Dreesmann and De Bijenkorf, or dream away in the sleepy Artis Zoo Aquarium. Small "personality" museums are the nicest places to be during such moments. Even the Rijksmuseum has some quiet departments left to visit with helpful gallery attendants.

A special treat for children is the doll-house department in the treasure-cellar of the Rijksmuseum. Children also like "their own" departments in the Van Gogh and Tropenmuseum (TM-Junior).

Other attractions on rainy days are a visit to the Heineken Brewery, Stadhouderskade or one of the nearby gem-cutting companies. Lacking mountains you can climb the Wester tower at the Westermarkt to take a view across the Jordaan, next to the Anne Frank House. Climbing excursions only take place during summertime. Rain or snow-free trips can be made by just taking a day-ticket for public transport.

There are only two — overground — metro lines in Amsterdam, connecting the new built Bijlmermeer with the Central Station. Every metro station has highly original décor. On your way to the metro-platforms of Central Station you can look through binoculars at the well-reproduced metro-paintings of Dutch artist Siet Zuyderland. He has painted the underground/metros of Moscow, Barcelona, London, Paris, New York, Tokyo, Vienna, Berlin etc.

MUSEUMS

Out of fifty museums the neighbouring Rijks-, Van Gogh, and Stedelijk Museum attract each year most foreign visitors.

Their popularity has much to do with the world-wide fame of the three considered-to-be most important Netherlandish artists: Rembrandt van Rijn, Vincent van Gogh and Piet Mondriaan (outside Holland known as Mondrian). Their work is part of the respective collections; Van Gogh is even represented in all three. The other Amsterdam museums show more or less the cultural and artistical background of Rembrandt, Vincent and Piet.

Nearly all museums sell a Museumkaart, a national museum-reduction pass which costs f 20,- and offers a whole year free entrance to over 250 Dutch museums. Without this pass you pay generally about f 5,- entry.

With a national Cultureel Jongeren Paspoort (Cultural Youth Passport), available for f 9,50, people between 15 and 25 years get reductions when visiting cultural events, while a museum-pass is included. (see: Cultural reduction passes).

Most museums are closed on Mondays, during Christmas, New Yearsday and on April 30th, Queensday.

Within each city zone an alphabetical delineation of their original Dutch names is given in this guide.

In this section the city is divided into the zones where most museums are located: between Jordaan-area and Dam-square, and the other one: the museum-area near Paulus Potterstraat and Stadhouderskade.

Finally, museums outside the centre are mentioned. Numbers refer to the map.

A short list of interesting museums of modern art elsewhere in Holland concludes the chapter.

Museum area
Area south of Spui and Muntplein, with southern canal-zone between Leidsegracht and Amstel-river including Museum-quarter. (Numbers refer to map).

Museum Fodor, Keizergracht 609, 'dam centrum. Telephone 249919/ 274306. Tram 16, 24, 25 (Vijzelstraat). *8*
Open Tue-Sat 10-5, Sundays and National holidays 1-5. Once used as department of the Stedelijk Museum, Fodor now has its own responsibility to show exhibitions of work by young, promising Amsterdam artists. Every summer Fodor, named after a wealthy nineteenth-century coal-merchant, shows the harvest of the art bought by the city of Amsterdam for its collection. Next to the exit Fodor's curators invite you to leave a critique in their book. Reading their reactions some visitors only seem to like the garden.

Van Gogh Museum, Paulus Potterstraat 7, A'dam zuid. Telephone 764881. Tram 2, 3, 5, 12, 16; bus 26 (Museumstraat van Baerlestraat). *38*
Open Tue-Sat 10-5, Sun 1-5. Vincent van Gogh, his life and his art hardly need further introduction. This Van Gogh Museum was formed in 1973 out of the collection of Vincent's nephew — the son of his brother Theo-Vincent Willem van Gogh. Architect Gerrit Rietveld played a major role in the design of the museum, although he died in 1964 long before it was finally built. The collection's paintings and drawings are presented chronologically, supplemented with quotes from Vincent's letters to Theo. First studies, clair-obscur paintings of the Brabant period, lead to the clear colours of French Provence in the dramatic painting with black crows above a yellow corn-field in Auvers-sur-Oise. Paintings by Monticelli, Bernard, and Gauguin, and Hokusai prints, which influenced Vincent's art, are also exhibited. The "potato-eaters" cannot be found here but in the Kröller Müller Museum in Otterlo (see: Museums outside Amsterdam).

In the back of the museum a workshop organises creative activities for visitors, amateur-artists and children.

Terrace of Vincent van Gogh museum

Museum van Loon, Keizersgracht 672, A'dam centrum. Telephone 245255. Tram 16, 24, 25 (Vijzelstraat). *6*
Only open on Monday from 10-12 and 1-4. Travel back to the 17th-Golden-century just by visiting Van Loon. Well preserved interiors, many portrait paintings of the family; mayors of Amsterdam. The first floor of the museum can be rented for (decadent) parties.

Rijksmuseum, Stadhouderskade 42, A'dam zuid. Telephone 732121. Tram 6, 7, 10, 16, 24, 25; bus 26 (Weteringschans, Museumstraat). *37*
Open Tue-Sat 10-5, Sundays and National Holidays 1-5. Some departments are closed in the afternoon, so ask the guards near the entrances (two, each side of the arch). The Rijksmuseum, home of Rembrandt's "Nightwatch" was built in 1885 by P. J. H. Cuypers. The collection of Dutch 17th century painting is regarded as one of the most important in the world. Represented painters of this "Golden century"are Rembrandt Harmensz van Rijn, Johannes Vermeer, Jan Steen, Frans Hals, Jan van Goyen, Aelbert Cuyp and Salomon Ruysdael.

The violation of Rembrandt's most famous painting "The corporal's rank of Frans Banning Cocq" (1653) better known by its nick-name "the Night-watch" tells something about its impact. Some visitors skate straight over the well-polished floors just to see this painting. Recently a special hall of honour has been rebuilt around the Nightwatch.

Other famous Rembrandts paintings are "the Jewish bride" and his moving "Self portrait as Paul". Another well-protected celebrity is Vermeer's "Milkmaid", which was stolen some years ago, but is now perfectly restored.

This excellent collection of Dutch art contains some works by older painters that are worth seeing: Geertgen tot Sint Jans, Jan van Scorel, both masters of the early "primitive" North-Netherlandish painting.

Elsewhere in the Rijks are sculptures, ceramics, textiles and interiors from the 12th to 20th century (art nouveau).

If you have more time to spend, you certainly must visit some hidden "highlights" in the back of the museum: the 18th-19th century department with some very fine Dutch (pre-) impressionist painting of Jongkind, Breitner, and Maris.

Netherlandish history — from the earliest days of our civilisation, colonial expansion, British-Dutch sea-battles, the Spanish, French and German occupation — is illustrated by paintings, documents, battered battle-flags and ship-models. Contemporary history is shown in temporary photograph-exhibitions.

The print-department, which you can enter through the right entrance, has regular shows of drawings from 15th-20th century, as well as Japanese prints (Utomaro, Hokusai etc).

At the rear-side of the Rijksmuseum the Asiatic Museum is hidden. Here you find Indian, Japanese, Chinese and Korean sculpture, pottery and paintings. Between these fine collections some attractive dollshouses, jewellery and early costumes are shown in the "treasure-cellar".

You may need at least a week to visit all the departments within the Rijksmuseum. But there's a nice old-fashioned buffet restaurant.

Stedelijk Museum, Paulus Potterstraat 13, A'dam zuid. Telephone 732166. Tram 2, 3, 5, 12; bus 26 (van Baerlestraat). *39*
Open Tue-Sat 10-5, Sundays and National Holidays 1-5. The Stedelijk (=Municipal) Museum Amsterdam can be regarded as one of the most

important in Europe. The building itself, however doesn't look as modern as the art exhibited inside. It was designed in 1895 by Dutch neo-renaissance architect A. W. Weismann. He intended to create it as an exhibition space for mainly historical paintings.

After 1920 the development of art changed this and contemporary artists were allowed to show their work here. It was however managing director Mr. Willem Sandberg who made radical changes after 1945. He decided to repaint the interior white and started using spans in the exhibition rooms. His talents as a typographer gave the lay-out of the catalogues and the posters of the Stedelijk a sober but clear modern face. Sandberg's (he died in 1984) major achievement was his introduction — in spite of all criticism — of the young, wild COBRA painters of the early fifties: Appel, Jorn, Corneille, Pedersen and Constant. Their work nowadays forms an important part of the collection. By doing this, Sandberg made way for the full development of Dutch modern art, explaining "he preferred young art, which doesn't want to please but only can cry like a new-born baby!"

Sandberg's successor Mr. Edy de Wilde turned out to be less revolutionary, but he introduced American pop and minimal-art, colourfield-painting and the Young Italians to Holland. Mr. Edy de Wilde, leader of the Stedelijk from 1963 to 1985 always remained faithful to the fine art of painting, avoiding art which couldn't be "understood by the eye". His fine personal choice was reflected in the La Grande Parade exhibition in 1985. Mr. Wim Beeren, former director of the Rotterdam Museum Boymans Van Beuningen, is Stedelijk's new director since February 1985. In Rotterdam and incidentally in Amsterdam he turned out to have original ideas about organizing exhibitions. It is believed Beeren will be more involved in current art-happenings.

Next to the Cobra part of the collection the unique Kasimir Malevitch collection is a very important part of the Stedelijk. Sandberg bought it in 1958, some thirty years after Malevitch himself composed this survey, showing his development from realism towards cubism. Older examples of early modern art are Van Gogh, Monet, Manet, Bonnard, Cézanne, Soutine, Picasso, Chagall (Fiddler on the Roof). German

New wing of the Stedelijk Museum

expressionists represented here are Kirchner, Schmidt-Rotluff and Max Beckmann. (Double-portrait with his wife Quappi, painted during his exile in Amsterdam on his atelier on the Rokin.)

De Stijl (=Style) painters and architects form another interesting part of the collection: Piet Mondrian (in Holland usually known as Mondriaan), Theo van Doesburg, Van der Leck and Gerrit Rietveld's furniture and a scale-model of the Schröder House (Utrecht). Of course Rietveld's famous red-blue-yellow (uncomfortable) wooden chair is on view here.

American visitors will enjoy the post-war American art of the Stedelijk. There are some fine abstract expressionist paintings by Willem De Kooning, who also presented some of his interesting little sculptures to the Museum. Warhol, Johns, Oldenburg, Rauschenberg, Rosenquist are the American pop-art representants. Colour-field painting fills the Hall of Honor, right above the marble stairs. Works by Newman, Stella, Kelly. Minimal art comes from the United States and the Netherlands: Ryman, Flavin, LeWitt, Schoonhoven, Visser, Struycken.

After visiting the excellent lunchroom you can join the eternal visitors in Edward Kienholz' horrifying Bar, next to the entrance of the Library.

European artists who share exhibition rooms are Bacon, Dubuffet, Martial Raysse, Gilbert & George, Merz, Klein, Beuys. Henri Matisse "La perruche et la sirène", the monumental gouache paper cut composition was bought in 1967, thanks to support of the Vereniging Rembrandt and the Prins Bernhard Fonds.

Interesting Dutch artists in the Stedelijk are Dibbets (photo-construction), Van Elk (photo-sculptures) and painters Armando, Van Velde, Schoonhoven, Westerik (Cut by grass) and more recently Daniëls, Verhoef, Content and Blom.

Latest developments in painting from Germany: Baselitz, Penck, Kiefer, Italy: Chia, Clemente, Cucchi and Paladino. Also young Julian Schabel from the United States is present there.

Sculptures by Rodin, Wouters, Couzijn, Serra, Henry Moore are shown in the garden. During summer you can enjoy the funny fountain mechanism of Jean Tinguely in front of the terrace. In the New Wing, overlooking the Van Baerlestraat artists' unions show their activities in rather dull exhibitions. The Stedelijk further includes small but interesting departments with photography, design, typography (Werkman), print and drawing room, halfway up the stairs. Downstairs you'll find the video-room.

Each Saturday and/or Sunday afternoon free concerts of contemporary modern music are held in the auditorium.

Universiteitsbibliotheek/Persmuseum/Schriftmuseum, Singel 425, A'dam centrum. Telephone 5252476. Tram 1, 2, 4, 5, 9, 16, 24, 25 (Spui/Rokin). *13*

Open Mon-Fri 11-1 and 2-4.30. Three small collections placed in the modern labyrinth built behind the old Militiegebouw-facade.

In the Persmuseum, which can be seen walking on street-level, is the history of the Dutch press since 1618, newspapers and cartoons can be seen.

On the second floor inside the building the museum of writing can be found. A one-man museum with clay-tablets, manuscripts on papyrus and other ancient writing-materials dating back to 3000 B.C.

On special request the curator leaves the room to show the paraphernalia of Dutch writers from the 17th and 20th century, Vondel, Van Eeden and Verwey.

17th century garden of Museum Willet Holthuysen on the Amstelstraat

Museum Willet-Holthuysen, Herengracht 605, A'dam centrum. Telephone 264290. Tram 4 (Rembrandtsplein). *10*
Open Tue-Sat 10-5, Sundays and National Holidays 1-5.
Hidden away from the business world and night-life round the Rembrandtsplein this little historical museum seems to keep memories alive. In this house lived generations of wealthy Amsterdam patricians. They left collections of ceramics, silver, glassworks and some authentic looking interiors overlooking a neo-classical garden on the Amstelstraat.

The horrifying sleeping-room at the second floor dates from the nineteenth century: here you can still imagine hearing the breathing of the last person who lived here, Mrs. Willet, who spent her days living in isolation, sharing a terrible Secret with innumerable cats.

Jordaan area
Area west of Dam-square and Muntplein, with western canal zone between Haarlemmerstraat and Leidsegracht including the Jordaan-quarter. (Numbers refer to map).

Allard Pierson Museum, Oude Turfmarkt 127, A'dam centrum. Telephone 5252556. Tram 4, 9, 14, 16, 24, 25 (Rokin/Spui). *38*
Open Tue-Fri 10-5, Saturday and Sunday and National Holidays 1-5. This archaeological museum belonging to Amsterdam University sometimes seems to be forgotten by foreign visitors, although most of them line up in front of it, awaiting their canal-trip.

Allard Pierson was a 19th century humanist who gave his name to this collection, housed in the former neo-classical Bank of the Netherlands.

Compared with the collections of the British Museum and the Louvre the Allard Pierson Museum is smaller and is more modest in character.

But the small statues from ancient Egypt, Greece and Rome are worth a visit. Also of interest are antique households, mummies, coins, arms, glassworks and jewellery from Western-Asia (Iraq, Iran, Syria, Palestine, Turkey), the Cretan and Cyprean Isles, Greece and the Roman Empire.

Interesting exhibitions about architecture, forgery, etc., are frequently organised by students and University lecturers.

Amstelkring, O. Z. Voorburgwal 40, A'dam centrum. Telephone 246604. Tram/bus/metro (Central Station, walk eastwards direction St. Nicolas Church). *42*
Open Mon-Sat 10-5, Sundays/National Holidays 1-5. "Our Good Lord Of The Attic" is a clandestine Catholic Church, from 1660, hidden in a house.

During the 16th and 17th century Catholicism was more or less forbidden by the North-Netherlandish Calvinists. Nowadays the museum houses this church, still used for weddings and divine services.

Interesting paintings from the 16th and 17th centuries are found inside, by De Keyser and De Bray.

Amsterdam Historisch Museum, Kalverstraat 92, A'dam centrum. Telephone 255822. Tram 1, 2, 4, 5, 14, 16, 24, 25 (N. Z. Voorburgwal/St. Luciënsteeg). *35*
Open Tue-Sat 10-5, Sundays/National Holidays 1-5. Near the shopping area round Kalverstraat and Spui passers-by drift into a covered street-gallery where portraits of the Amsterdam civic guards are on display.

This gallery is part of the Historical Museum, in which till 1960 orphans were raised and cared for.

Many paintings, tools and pottery are shown, related to the history of the city, which 700 years ago was built around a dam in the river Amstel (Amstelredam). The earliest part of the collection dates back to the 13th century and ends up in our own time. Nearly every year archaeologists find traces of old Amsterdam, hidden underneath a demolished building in the city.

In the restaurant tall visitors can shake hands with the biblical giant Goliath, while David plus assistant admire your courage.

Architectuur museum, Droogbak 1a, A'dam centrum. Telephone 220277. Bus 18, 22 (Haarlemmerstraat or walk westwards from Central Station). *55*
Open Mon-Fri 10-5, closed weekends. Irregular exhibitions. The highly unconventional exterior of the architecture museum is designed in the "Amsterdam School" style by P. Marnette in 1925. (see also: Architectural interest). Inside, temporary events are held about construction-design, with scale-models and photographs from the personal archives of famous Dutch architects Berlage, Cuypers, Oud and Duyker. The latter two were represented in the De 8/Opbouw magazine.

Bijbels museum, Herengracht 366, A'dam centrum. Telephone 247949. Tram 1, 2, 5 (Leidsestraat). *25*
Open Tue-Sat 10-5, Sundays and National Holidays 1-5. Biblical museum with objects and texts from countries related to the Holy Book.

Fonografisch museum, Elandsgracht 111, A'dam centrum. Telephone 230471. Tram 7, 10, 13, 17; bus 65, 66, 67 (Marnixstraat/Police Office). *3*
Open Mon-Fri 11-5, Saturdays 9-5, closed on Thursdays and Sundays. Set up by an enthusiastic gramophone-collector in 1982. An interesting, nostalgic museum with scenic background-music, where the first Edison Phonograph (1877), the Emile Berliner Gramophone (1883) — an ancestor of the contemporary stereo-set — as well as new hi-fi developments can be admired.

On Saturdays at the neighbouring auction-hall other interesting second hand cameras and gramophones can be bought.

Anne Frank Huis, Prinsengracht 263, A'dam centrum. Telephone 264533. Tram 13, 14, 17; bus 21 (Westermarkt). *19*
Open Mon-Sat 9-5, Sundays and National Holidays 10-5. Anne Frank was a 15-year-old Jewish girl, who died in the concentration-camp Bergen-Belsen, some time before its liberation in 1945. The every-day life she and her family were forced to live here in the house, hidden behind a cupboard, before their arrest by the Gestapo in 1944 is described in her moving diary.

Apart from showing the practical souvenirs of this period, which keeps her memory alive the Anne Frank Foundation primarily organizes temporary exhibitions on actual examples of racism, fascism and anti-semitism. The museum itself is constantly crowded with many visitors from all parts of the world; a strange development, for this anonymous canal-house really was for some time a secret and safe hiding-place.

Madame Tussaud, Kalverstraat 156, A'dam centrum. Telephone 229449. Tram 1, 2, 4, 5, 14, 16, 24, 25 (Rokin/Spui). *34*
Open daily from 10-6, from July till September 10-8. A well-known attraction with wax personalities. By visiting this Amsterdam feature you can find out the international and national "who's who in Holland". Dutch artists are represented by Rembrandt in his clair-obscur studio (awaiting divine inspiration perhaps) and contemporary Cobra-painter Karel Appel. You can wander through Jeroen Bosch' garden of delight, but don't touch. Piet Mondrian is not present, so let's suggest they add a wax image of him, dancing to jazzy tunes in his New York or Paris atelier; and where is Van Gogh cutting off his ear?

Nederlands Theater Instituut, Herengracht 166, A'dam centrum. Telephone 235104. Tram 13, 14 (Raadhuisstraat). *49*
Open Tue-Fri 10-5, Saturday and Sunday 11-5. Located in a classic canal-house, the Theatre Institute organizes exhibitions on subjects connected with the dramatic arts and cabaret on stage or television. Costumes, posters, prints, texts, scale-stages and video tapes bring back unforgettable nights at the opera.

Koninklijk Paleis, Dam, A'dam centrum. Telephone 248698. Tram 1, 2, 4, 5, 9, 13, 14, 16, 17, 24, 25; bus 21. *44*
Open mostly every afternoon from 1.30-4. The Amsterdam residence of Her Majesty the Queen Beatrix of the Netherlands, who only lives here on special occasions.

Visitors are invited to admire the 17th century masterpiece of Jacob van Campen. Inside are decorative paintings by Bol, Dou, Flinck, who were all students of Rembrandt. Rembrandt's own painting: "The oath of the Batavians" was refused and now can be seen in the Stockholm National Museum. The Royal Palace was first used as a Town Hall and residence during the French Occupation by Lodewijk Napoleon, brother of the Emperor. The Empire-style of this period is the important style up until today. A contemporary historic place of interest is the *Mozeszaal* where in 1980 former Queen Juliana signed the act of abdication in favour of her daughter Beatrix.

Every second week of October Queen Beatrix invites young Dutch painters to show their work in the palace for the Royal Grant of 5000 guilders. This exhibition serves as a spring-board for the careers of young artists.

Spaarpottenmuseum, Raadhuisstraat 20, A'dam centrum. Telephone 221066. Tram 13, 14; bus 21. *45*
Open Mon-Fri 1-4. A museum to save for a rainy day; set up by a former

bank-manager. Piggy-banks that survived the hammer, mechanical saving-banks, and kitsch and art are gathered together.

Universiteit van Amsterdam: Historische collectie, O. Z. Voorburgwal 231, A'dam centrum. Telephone 5253339. Tram/bus walk from Central Station, direction St. Nicolaas Church. *40*
Open Mon-Fri 9-5. Books, clippings, prints, photographs and other souvenirs of the over-300-year-old Amsterdam University, are now housed in a former monastery.

MUSEUMS OUTSIDE THE CENTRE OF THE CITY

Aviodome, Schiphol Airport. Telephone 173640. Bus CN 143, 144, 145.
Open daily from 10-5, closed on Sundays between 1 November and 1 April. There is a new train link now from Leiden. The first museum for your children to visit when you arrive by plane in Amsterdam. Aviodome, housed in a futuristic looking hemispherical hall, shows the development of aeronautica. Also helicopters, Link trainers and recent space-shuttles are here. Of course Anthony Fokker, the Dutch aeroplane pioneer, has not been forgotten.

Bosmuseum, Koenenkade, Amsterdamse Bos. Bus 70 (only summer) or old-time tramway from Haarlemmermeer-station, Amstelveenseweg.
Open Mon-Fri 9-5, weekends 10-5. In the middle of the Amsterdamse Bos Park this museum deals with the history of the park, which was some fifty years ago created by unemployed labourers by means of a Dutch version of the American New Deal policy.

Busmuseum/Museum-tramlijn, Haarlemmermeerstration, Amstelveenseweg 264, A'dam zuid. Telephone 790078. Tram 16; bus 15, 23, 60.
Open by appointment only. Old time buses once driven through parts of Holland during the early fifties and sixties. From this former railway station you can take a ride on a historic tramway to the Amsterdamse Bos, Amstelveen, and Uithoorn. The tram runs in the summer period 1st April-28th October from 10-6 only on Sundays, and during 2 June-1 September also on Saturday from 12-6. The tram-cars are generally 50 years old, and the trip takes half an hour following the ancient railway to Amstelveen, passing Olympic Stadium, Amsterdamse Bos and De Poel, a small lake near Bovenkerk.

Gemeentelijke Archiefdienst, Amsteldijk 67, A'dam zuid. Telephone 763131. Tram 3-4 (van Woustraat or Ceintuurbaan).
Former town hall of Nieuweramstel (now called Amstelveen) with the archives of famous citizens, streets, etc. Temporary exhibitions are held with topographical drawings and paintings or photographs of Amsterdam. In the archives Amsterdam citizens can trace back their ancestry.

Geologisch museum, Nieuwe Prinsengracht 130, A'dam centrum. Telephone 5222830. Tram 6, 7, 10, 14; bus 56; metro (Wibautstraat).
Rocks, minerals, prehistoric fossils form the collection of Amsterdam University Geological Museum.

Joods Historisch museum, Nieuwmarkt 4, A'dam centrum. Telephone 269945/253388, metro (Nieuwmarkt).
Open Tue-Sat 10-5, Sundays and National Holidays 1-5. Amsterdam acquired its nickname Mokum — Yiddish equivalent of "large city" — after becoming a second home for Jewish refugees since the 16th century. With their own cultural history, the Jewish customs and traditional

celebrations are shown in this Waaggebouw, the former Weigh-building. Between Nieuwmarkt and Weesperstraat was the Jewish Quarter, before being cleared out by the Nazis during WW II. Documents and photographs remind us of this tragic period. Also exhibitions of work by international Jewish artists and designers are held here.

NINT Technisch museum, Tolstraat 129, A'dam zuid. Telephone 646021. Tram 3, 4 (van Woustraat).
Open Mon-Fri 10-4, weekends 1-5. Exhibitions on the basic principles of science, transport, photography, energy, telecommunication, electronics and computers form together the Technical Museum in the Tolstraat near the river Amstel. Texts, photographs and working-models demonstrate the development of modern technology.

This museum, housed in a former gem-cutting factory, is recommended for a visit with older children, who are allowed to use all the equipment.

Peter Stuyvesant Stichting, Drentestraat 21, A'dam Buitenveldert. Telephone 5406911. Bus 23 (De Boelelaan).
Open Mon-Fri 9-10 and 1-4, preferably by appointment. Exhibition-space in the office building of a large British-American tobacco company. Generally abstract post WW II art with paintings and sculptures by Karel Appel, Bram Bogart, Niki de St. Phalle, Tajiri etc. On special request a film is shown. The works of art circulate here and in the cigarette-factory in Zevenaar, near the Dutch-German border in Gelderland.

Rembrandthuis, Jodenbreestraat 4-6, A'dam centrum. Telephone 249486. Tram 9-14 (Valckeniersstraat/Mozes en Aäronkerk) metro (Nieuwmarkt).
Open Mon-Sat 10-5, Sundays and National Holidays 1-5. Sometimes people mix this Rembrandt-house up with the Rijksmuseum, as no "Rembrandt-museum" exists in Amsterdam. Although born in Leiden, where only the facade of his birth-house near the Galgewater is still standing, Rembrandt spent most of his life in Amsterdam. Somewhere beneath the floor of the Westerkerk the remains of this great artist are buried. From 1639 till 1660 Rembrandt lived here in the (then called) Breestraat, the Jewish Quarter of the City. Later he moved to houses on the Rozengracht and Bloemgracht, in the Jordaan quarter. Nowadays most of his 250 etchings are on display in the Rembrandthuis.

Each last Sunday of the month (from September till April) a printmaker demonstrates the noble etching technique, reminding the visitors of the 19th century when Rembrandt was regarded only as an important printmaker.

After visiting the Rembrandthuis you can walk straight to the Waterlooplein fleamarket, or Waaggebouw on Nieuwmarkt.

Nederlands Scheepvaartmuseum, Kattenburgerplein 1, A'dam centrum. Telephone 254175; bus 22, 28.
Open Tue-Sat 10-5, Sundays 1-5. Near the IJ harbour Amsterdam's maritime history took place. Voyages to the East and West Indies brought Holland the prosperity of the 17th or Golden century, positively influencing the development of Dutch art. In the Shipping-museum, a former marine-warehouse from the Verenigde Oostindische Compagnie, ship-models from these and more recent centuries are shown. The collection

includes an authentic sailship and steamer, which can be seen outside the museum and contains some very fine marine-paintings by the famous Willem van de Velde and Andreas Schotel. Ship-lovers will also like the Krombout wharf (see below) and the biennial "Sail Amsterdam" regatta when ships of all ages visit the IJ harbour, taking us back to a time when Holland ruled the waves. The next Sail Amsterdam is in 1985, then 1987.

Tropenmuseum/Kindermuseum TM Junior, Linnaeusstraat 2, A'dam oost. Telephone 652680. Tram 3, 6, 9, 10 (Mauritskade).
Open Mon-Fri 10-5, Sundays and Holidays 12-5. A recently rebuilt museum with a special interest in the third world as well as in the position of immigrants from North-Africa and Southern-Europe who now live and work here.

A life-size village with authentic background noises gives the impression that you really somewhere in Bombay.

Children have a special museum within the Tropenmuseum: the TM Junior, where they can play, cook, and eat special exotic dishes.

In the auditorium performances of non-Western music and dances are held every Sunday, as well as regular film-sessions.

Werf 't Krombout, Hoogte Kadijk 147, A'dam east. Telephone 276777. Bus 22, 28 (mill near Czaar Peterstraat).
Open Mon-Fri 10-4, closed during weekends and holidays. The wharf, where steamers were built is now a nice place to chat to amateur-sailors who restore their traditional boats here. Small museum.

Zöologisch museum, Plantage Middeblaan 53, A'dam east. Telephone 5223624. Tram 6, 7, 10, 9, 14 (Artis Zoo).
Open Tue-Sun 9.30-4.30, but closed Saturday. Collection of skeletons and bones of similar animals who are alive and well in the nearby Artis Zoo. Recommended for people who like to make sketches à la Henry Moore. Also diorama with sad-looking stuffed animals in eternal dune-landscape.

Zeiss Planetarium, Kromwijkdreef 11, A'dam Bijlmermeer. Telephone 963484. Metro-terminal Gaasperplas.
Observatory of the heavenly bodies, combined with an attractive audio-visual show to make you wonder about the possible life among the sun and moon and other astronomical phenomena.

Specially opened to watch solar/lunar eclipse.

After visiting the planetarium or space-shuttle passes you can walk through the large Floriade-park (constructed for a large horticultural show), fortunately without strange looking green men: only the grass and the leaves are green!

MUSEUMS OUTSIDE AMSTERDAM

The things you miss in Amsterdam museums you will possibly find elsewhere in the country of Holland. The Dutch "Open station" system (tickets inspected on the trains and clipped, so stop off as often as you like on the way) means that visitors from Britain arriving by boat at the Hook of Holland or Vlissingen, French visitors from Paris, or Belgian visitors from Brussels or Antwerp will find themselves on the main line which passes through art cities such as Rotterdam, Delft, the Hague (Den Haag or 's Gravenhage), Leiden and Haarlem on the way to Amsterdam so they can gorge themselves on museums before they even arrive at Amsterdam. And of course Amsterdammers can do this in reverse order. Any town in Holland fits comfortably into a day trip from Amsterdam. Groningen is perhaps however just that little bit further away from Amsterdam.

ROTTERDAM

Museum Boymans-van Beuningen, Mathenesserlaan 18-20, Rotterdam. Telephone 010-361405. Tram 5 from Rotterdam Central Station. Open 10-5, closed on Monday, Sundays open 11-5. Founded in 1935 the Rotterdam museum joins both the historical and modern art collections of Mr. Boymans and Mr. Van Beuningen. Art from the Middle-Ages up till the 17th century includes paintings by: Hubert and Jan van Eyck, Hans Memlinc, Bouts, Jeroen Bosch, Bruegel, Frans, Hals, Saenredam (famous church-interior painter), Ruisdael and Rembrandt (portrait of his son Titus as monk). Modern painting by Klee, Jawlensky, Munch, Kandinsky and Dutch/French artist Kees van Dongen (fauvist). Boymans art section is sometimes regarded as an opponent of the Stedelijk, because of the surrealists, which are not on display in Amsterdam. Here you'll find De Chirico, Ernst, a lot of Magritte works and Dali's "Venus-with-drawers". Recently more work by Dali and Magritte was bought from the illustrious Edward James Collection. Next to surrealism also magic-realism by Belgian and Dutch artists Hynckes, Toorop, Koch and Willink. Other post-war art from Europe comes from Francis Bacon and Dutch artists Daniels, Schoonhoven, van Amen, Appel and Constant. Don't miss the poetic "tempera"-paintings by Co Westerik, a Rotterdam based artist, whose work is also shown by the Fenna de Vries gallery next to the museum.

More contemporary is the pop-art and minimal art collection from the USA: Oldenburg, Lewitt, Warhol and new trans-avant garde like Haring, Schnabel, Salle. The Amsterdam Stedelijk presented the Young Italians in Holland, and later on the Boymans' showed the works of the Young German Muelheimer Freihett: Salomé, Dahn. Jörg Immendorf; Ansel Kiefer and George Baselitz from an older generation painters from the Bundes republik. There are also interesting current Rotterdam art exhibitions and a large garden with post war sculpture.

The Rotterdamse Kunststichting, Rotterdam Art Foundation organises interesting contemporary art events at Galerie Westersingel 6 and Galerie 't Venster Oude Binnenweg 113. Information: 010 363111.

DELFT

Delft is a well-preserved 17th century town, with small scenic canals in the centre. Famous because of Johannes Vermeer van Delft but no Vermeer paintings to be found here, however. Every year in Museum Het Prinsenhof the Arts & Antiques Fair takes place in Delft.

In The Prinsenhof King Willem van Oranje "Father of the Fatherlands" was killed in 1584. Nowadays a bullet-hole near the stairs reminds us of this tragic murder.

Next to this hole, portrait-paintings from the 17th century are shown. You'll find The Prinsenhof, Agathaplein 1. Telephone 015-13311. Daily opened 10-5, Sundays 1-5.

THE HAGUE (DEN HAAG)

Mauritshuis, Binnenhof, The Hague is temporarily closed until about . . . so you have to look at Potters "Bull"" and Rembrandts "Anatomical lesson of Dr. Nicolaas Tulp" during the exchange exhibition in the Grand Palais in Paris in the spring of 1986. (see: Paris Art Guide by Fiona Dunlop)

Haags Gemeentemuseum, Stadhouderslaan 41, The Hague. Telephone 070-514181. Bus 4 from Central Station or tram 10 from the railway station Hollands Spoor.
Open Tue-Fri 10-5, Sundays and holidays 1-5. Museum built in 1929 by H. P. Berlage, one of Holland's major architects. The collection contains Dutch impressionists of the "Haagse School", fresh "plein-air" paintings and watercolours by Israels, Weissenbruch, Maris.

The most important part of the collection is the work of Piet Mondrian. Early figurative studies of the Gein river, finally transforming tree-forms, end up in the well-known red-blue-yellow abstract paintings, created according to the principles of De Stijl. More De Stijl members represented are Doesburg, Huszar, Van der Leck and Gerrit Rietveld. Other 20th century art to be found here: Jawlensky, Kandinsky, Léger, Moderssohn-Becker, Picasso, Moholy-Nagy, El Lissitsky, Max Ernst.

The museum also houses some very interesting style-interiors, design, ceramics, glass-works and a surprising department of old European and non-Western musical instruments from Africa, Oceania, Asia and Latin-America.

Panorama Mesdag, Zeestraat 65B, Den Haag. Telephone 070-642563. Bus 4 and 22, tram 7 from Central Station or bus 5, tram 8 from Hollandsch Spoor station.
Open 10-5 (March-October) and 10-4 (November/December) and 10-3 (January/February). The peculiar opening-hours of the Panorama are a result of the available daylight, important for the monumental painting inside. It shows Scheveningen, the sea and the beach and was painted by Hague School Impressionist H. W. Mesdag, his wife, and their colleagues De Bock and George Breitner. A curious museum to visit when you have time to spare in The Hague.

LEIDEN
Stedelijk museum de Lakenhal, Oude Singel 28-32, Leiden. Telephone 071-254933, walk from station.
Open 10-5, Sunday 1-5. Leiden is the oldest university-town in Holland. Therefore many interesting 19th century collections are to be found here. The Lakenhal (Cloth Hall) houses the city's most famous painter Lucas van Leyden "Last Judgment" triptych (15th century). Next to that 17th century paintings and sculptures by Rembrandt, Steen, Dou, Van Goyen. There is also a small modern art department.

The Rijksmuseum van Oudheden (Archeological museum), Rapenburg 28, 15 minutes walk from the station. Telephone 071-146246.
Open 10-5, Sundays 1-5. Greek, Roman, European pre-historic archeology.

The Rijksmuseum voor Volkenkunde (Ethnographical museum), Steenstraat 1. Telephone 071-132641. 5 minutes walk from the station.
Open 10-5, Sundays 1-5. Interesting collection with arts and crafts from all parts of the world, specially East-Asian, pre-Columbian and East-African Art.

More museums are to be found round Steenstraat, Rapenburg (near university-buildings) and Kerkstraat.

HAARLEM

Frans Halsmuseum, Groot Heiligland 62, Haarlem. Telephone 023-319180.
Open Mon-Sat 11-5, Sundays and National Holidays 1-5. Pleasant museum in former Elderly Persons' Home, where during the 17th century master-painter Frans Hals spent the last years of his life, old and slightly disappointed. As a kind of therapy the managers ordered him to paint a picture of them. The revolutionary lush-brushed paintings he made on this occasion are the chefs d'oeuvres of his career. Next to this some beautiful portraits by his contemporary Johannes Verspronck, and an interesting post-war modern art department, complete the Frans Hals museum.

Teylers museum, Spaarne 16, Haarlem. Telephone 023-320197. Bus 2, 5, 71 from Haarlem railway station.
Open Tue-Sat 10-5 (March-September) and every first Sunday of the month 1-5 (March-September) and open Tue-Sat 10-4 (October-February) and every first Sunday of the month 1-4. Teylers — named after a wealthy cloth-merchant — contains the oldest exhibition space in the Netherlands, the so-called Ovalen Zaal (Oval Room).

Typical 18-19th century collection of arts and sciences: geology, mineralogy and technical inventions. Art collection includes the complete graphic works of Rembrandt van Rijn and Romantic School painting (Koekoek, Kruseman, Springer, Allebé, Schelfhout). Behind the curtains see the master drawings by Claude Lorrain, Michelangelo and Raphael.

ARNHEM, OTTERLO

Rijksmuseum Kröller-Müller, National Park De Hoge Veluwe, Otterlo. Telephone 08382-241, take Hoge Veluwe bus from Arnhem station.
Open Tue-Sat 10-5, Sundays 1-5. A most impressive collection of Van Gogh paintings and drawings and also some other fine impressionists and expressionists from France and Holland, such as Breitner, Maris, Corot, Courbet, Redon, Rops, Denis, Seurat, Signac, Toorop. Cubists Picasso, Gris, Braque. Futurists Balla, Boccioni. De Stijl: Mondrian and interesting Bart van der Leck-collection.

Inside the Kröller-Müller and outside in the natural beauty of the forest reserve of the Hoge Veluwe a highly important collection of modern sculpture is exhibited. Represented are Rodin, Maillol, Marini, Moore, Caro, King, Dubuffet and more recently Fontana, André Volten, Serra, Christo, Panamarenko, Merz, Nauman, Long and the interesting Dutch sculptors Carel Visser and Henk Visch. Special collections of Barbara Hepworth, Hans Arp and Jacques Lipchitz, as well as primitive African and Polynesian sculpture make a special trip to Otterlo worthwhile.

The museum itself is placed in the natural beauty of the forest reserve of the Hoge Veluwe.

Gemeenetmuseum, Utrechtseweg 87, Arnhem. Telephone 085-512431. 10 minutes walk from the station.
Open 10-5, Sundays from 11-5. A small, friendly museum with its own lush atmosphere, which only can be a result of its location near the ever flowing Rijn river. Above in the exhibition-space art competes with the beauty of the winding river outside. The collection includes neo-realistic

Dutch and Belgian art by Hynckes, Mankes, Diek Ket, Carel Willink and Schuhmacher. During the young leadership of Mrs. Liesbeth Brandt Corstius the museum bought many new interesting art-works: Lucassem, Freymuth, Charlotte Mutsaers (wood-cuts), van der Haak, Maia Beatriz, Visser, Veneman, Veldhoen (all three of them with forms of new sculpture).

EINDHOVEN
Van Abbe museum, Bilderdijklaan 10, Eindhoven. Telephone 040-389730. Bus 4 from railway-station, direction "Kunstijsbaan" (stadhuis). Open Tue-Sat 10-5, Sundays and National Holidays 1-5. The industrial development of Eindhoven, some 115 kms south of Amsterdam resulted in Holland's famous Philips bulb-factory, but also in a cultural explosion.

The small Van Abbe museum, near the town hall of Eindhoven presents highly interesting avant-garde art expositions next to its own small post war painting and sculpture collection.

Curators of the Van Abbe organised the Dokumenta exhibition 1982 in Kassel (West Germany). Among represented artists are: Picasso, Beckmann, Mondrian, Kokoschka, Bracque, Lissitsky and more recently Penck, Tapiès, Gilbert & George, Tuttle, Broodthaers, Kiefer, Kounellis, Polke. Contemporary Dutch artists are Toon Verhoef, Henk Visch, René Daniels, Jan Schoonhoven, Jan Dibbets. In the city of Eindhoven some alternative art-spaces organise their own exhibitions: *Apollohuis, De Fabriek.* Between exhibitions the Van Abbe generally closes, so check before travelling to Eindhoven.

GRONINGEN
Groninger Museum voor Stad en Lande, Praediniussingel 59, Groningen. Telephone 050-172929. Walk 5 minutes from station.
Open Tue-Sat 10-5, Sundays 1-5. Up north and east in the Netherlands you'll find the province Groningen with its capital-town, bearing the same name. Like the museums in Arnhem and Eindhoven the Groningen Museum presents rather obstinate exhibitions from time to time. Home-collection contains paintings and drawings by Rembrandt and Carel Fabritius. Specialisation of the museum however is German expressionism and the local counterpart: De Ploeg-groep (plough) Managing director Mr. Frans Haks also presents highly contemporary art here, for instance making interesting shows with Henk Visch (sculptures), Clemente and recently Julian Opie with his "junk-art" sculptures.

Other Museums
Other interesting museums you'll find in Venlo, Maastricht (Limburg province), Utrecht, Amersfoort (Utrecht province) and Den Bosch (province Noord-Brabant, on your way to Eindhoven).

All Dutch museums are listed in *De Nederlandse Museumgids,* written by *Rudi Molegraaf,* edited by De Staatsuitgeverij and can be obtained in most museums.

ANTIQUES & ART DEALERS

Traditionally Amsterdam attracts collectors of prints, pre-1900 arts and crafts, but also people who are interested in more expensive curiosities, just for the sake of nostalgia.

Both groups visit a specific part of the city. The first-class antique-dealers are concentrated behind well protected doors around the Rokin and Dam-square.

In the area around the Rijksmuseum similar but smaller antique and simple curiosity shops conduct their business; walking from Spiegelgracht to Nieuwe Spiegelstraat, passing Prinsengracht or Herengracht you find shops with specialised trade, varying from old toys to ancient scientific and medical instruments.

More popular "antique", second hand utensils like gramophones, cameras, ceramics etc are sold next to the Phonographic Museum in the antique-hall of the Looiersgracht: de Looier.

Listed below are the art and antique-dealers selling pre-1900 arts and crafts. Most of them are one-man shops, with their own opening-hours, so it's wise to phone before visiting a specific antique-dealer.

Old print shop, Spiegelgracht

MUSEUM AREA BETWEEN SPIEGELGRACHT AND LEIDSESTRAAT, including the connecting Kerkstraat. Tram 6, 7, 10 (Weteringschans).

Aalderink, Spiegelgracht 15, A'dam centrum. Telephone 230211.
Asiatic art, ethnographics.

Agora, Cornelis Schuytstraat 9, A'dam zuid. Telephone 799234.
Art-nouveau, art-déco and other 18-19th century crafts also children's books.

Amsterdam Antique Gallery, Nieuwe Spiegelstraat 34, A'dam centrum. Telephone 253371.
Thirteen antiquarians. Russian icons, some 17-19th century painting and prints.

Art gallery Amsterdam, Leidsestraat 57, A'dam centrum. Telephone 244225.
Classic and modern painting, miniatures.

Arts connected 1900-1960, Kerkstraat 123, A'dam centrum. Telephone 245360.
Prints, paintings from 1900-1960, as name of the antique dealer indicates. Graphic works by Léger, Matisse and Japanese "ukiyo-e" woodcuts by Toyokuni, Ei-Sen. Also Jugendstil and contemporary paintings.
Next to all that is some fine "New Objectivity" furniture.

Astanmangala, Kerkstraat 165, A'dam centrum. Telephone 234402.
Tibetan, Indian miniatures, ethnographics.

Blitz, Nieuwe Spiegelstraat 37A, A'dam centrum. Telephone 232663.
Asiatic arts and crafts.

Brinkman, Nieuwe Spiegelstraat 30, A'dam centrum. Telephone 274466.
Incidental 18th and 19th century paintings available.

Fijnaut, Nieuwe Spiegelstraat 31, A'dam centrum. Telephone 256374.
Garden-statues, China from the Hatcher Collection, 17-19th century paintings from Holland, Flanders and France: Droog, De Gruyter, Voyant, Cossard, Verhoeven.

Gasseling, Nieuwe Spiegelstraat 66, A'dam centrum. Telephone 231002.
Judaica.

Elisabeth v.d. Nes, Nieuwe Spielgracht 44, A'dam centrum. Telephone 261012.
20th century Dutch expressionists of De Bergensche School.

Leidelmeyer, Nieuwe Spiegelstraat 58, A'dam centrum. Telephone 254627.
Art déco, art-nouveau, tea-sets by Lalique a.o.

Lemaire, Reguliersgracht 80, A'dam centrum. Telephone 237027.
Asiatic arts, ethnographics.

C. F. A. Roelofsz, Leidsegracht 42, A'dam centrum. Telephone 255568.
Tram 1, 2, 5 (Leidsestraat).
Dutch 17th century painting, French impressionists and major other art-styles.

Mr. H. Schlichte Bergen, P. C. Hooftstraat 53, A'dam zuid. Telephone 793005. Tram 2, 3, 5, 12 (van Baerlestraat); bus 26, 65, 66 (Stadhouderskade).
Medieval sculpture and paintings. P. C. Hooftstraat is one of the most exclusive shopping-streets in Amsterdam.

Drs.J. H. Schlichte Bergen, Velazquezstraat 8, A'dam zuid. Telephone 769344. Tram 5; bus 60, 65, 67 (Beethovenstraat/Stadionkade).
Between Rubensstraat and Holbeinstraat, both aside of the Stadionkade lies the Velazquezstraat. Old master paintings.

C. M. Kooring-Verwindt, Spiegelgracht 14-16, A'dam centrum. Telephone 236538.
Post-war painting by Van Velde, Alechinsky, Daniëls.

A. van der Gulik, Nieuwe Spiegelstraat 37, A'dam centrum. Telephone 240322.
Asiatic arts and crafts.

Hendriks, Nieuwe Spiegelstraat 61, A'dam centrum. Telephone 230085.
19-20th century painting, prints, drawings by Dutch Marius Bauer, Schelfhout, Gestel, Roelofs, Gabriel, Haagse School-painters, Romantic School.

Rob Kattenburg, De Lairessestraat 96, A'dam zuid. Telephone 622337. Tram 16.
Dutch and English marine-painting from 16-19th century: Koekoek, Hulk, Cooke, Smit.

AREA AROUND ROKIN AND DAM SQUARE.
Tram 4, 9, 14, 16, 24, 25.

Bunschoten, Staalkade 2, A'dam centrum. Telephone 244295. Tram 4-9 (Amstel).
Pre-Columban art.

P. de Boer, Herengracht 512, A'dam centrum. Telephone 236849/231285.
Hollandish and Flemish master painting from 15-17th century: Camphuysen, Jan van Goyen, etcetera.

Gebroeders Douwes, Rokin 46, A'dam centrum. Telephone 236208.
Dutch, Flemish 17th century, Dutch, French 19th century painting, drawings, prints. Major Amsterdam antiquair, also London branch: 38 Duke Street, St James. Telephone 01-839 5795.

Kunstzalen A. Vecht, Rokin 30, A'dam centrum. Telephone 234748.
Asiatic arts, sculpture, bronzes, archeology.

K. & V. Waterman, Rokin 116, A'dam centrum. Telephone 232958.
French and Dutch 19th century painting.

M. Hart, Rokin 122, A'dam centrum. Telephone 231658.
16-19th century topographic engravings and prints.

Bernard Houthakker, Rokin 98, A'dam centrum. Telephone 233939.
Fine collection of master drawings from 15-20th century by various artists. Also sculpture, painting.

Morpurgo, Rokin 108, A'dam centrum. Telephone 235883.
Sculptures, bronzes, china, glass, furniture, Asiatic arts.

Prestige Art Gallery, Reguliersbreestraat 46, A'dam centrum. Telephone 240104.
17-20th century painting and bronzes.

Salomon Stodel Antiquité, Rokin 70, A'dam centrum. Telephone 231692.
18th century French painting, tapestries, sculpture.

Magdalene Sothmann/Johannes Marcus, Nieuwe Zijds Voorburgwal 284, A'dam centrum. Telephone 236920. Tram 1, 2, 5.
Japanese and 18-20th century prints, also contemporary art-gallery, recently re-opened with exposition of drawings by Otto Dix.

JORDAAN QUARTER
Tram 13, 14, 17 (Westermarkt).

Paul Cassirer, Keizersgracht 109, A'dam centrum. Telephone 248337.
Paintings, drawings, etchings of various centuries.

Ex-Coenders, Keizersgracht 150, A'dam centrum. Telephone 255180.
Old Samplers.

An **Art Antique fair** is held every October/November in the **Museum Het Prinsenhof** in **Delft**, a presentation and exhibition of major Dutch antiquarians, and also during Amsterdam Art week every March in the Nieuwe Kerk, Dam Square.

Auction-houses

All Amsterdam auction-houses have regular view-days, auctions and publish Dutch/English catalogues. Listed below are the auction-houses, dealing with all important old and modern paintings, prints, antique furniture, Chinese and English china, sculptures, old and contemporary arts and crafts. Also valuations.

Paul Brandt, Keizersgracht 738, A'dam centrum. Telephone 248662/230301. Tram 4 (Utrechtsestraat).
Renowned Dutch auction-house, also organising contemporary and traditional art exhibitions.

Christie's Amsterdam, Cornelis Schuytstraat 57, A'dam zuid. Telephone 642011. Tram 16 (De Lairessestraat).
Continental branch of the British famous international auction-house, housed in the former Shipping-museum near the Amsterdam Hilton Hotel.

Sothebys, Mak van Waay, Rokin 102, A'dam centrum. Telephone 246215/243188. Tram 4, 16, 24, 25.
International auction-house. Scenic view-days on dull Sundays on Rokin and Nes. Sometimes very interesting presentations with Dutch 18th and 19th century Romantic and Impressionist painters. Regular contemporary graphics by Maurits Escher (trompe-l'oeil lithographs), Freymuth, Westerik.

De Zwaan, Keizersgracht 474, A'dam centrum. Telephone 220447. Tram 1, 2, 5 (Leidsestraat).
Managing-director Dr. G. van den Brink. Auctions of old furniture and less exclusive antique arts and crafts. (Zwaan is Dutch for Swan).

Van Gendt, Keizersgracht 96-98, A'dam centrum. Telephone 234107/234157. Tram 1, 2, 5, 13, 17 (Westermarkt/N. Z. Voorburgwal).
Interesting book-auctions; also paintings, prints, maps and drawings by Escher, Filarski, Schuhmacher.

De Zon, Singel 118, A'dam centrum. Telephone 240432/233558. Tram 1, 2, 5, 13 (N. Z. Voorburgwal, Post Office).
Fa. Loth Gijselman. Art, antiques and second hand furniture.

Exhibition before auction at Sothebys, Mak van Waay's, Nes

COMMERCIAL GALLERIES

Some Amsterdam gallery dealers claim the large number of modern art galleries to be the result of the late sixties and early seventies, when art-buying was supported by the Dutch government.

The tradition of antique-dealers created a good atmosphere for the now over fifty Amsterdam galleries. Nevertheless not all these galleries can be regarded as serious enterprises; therefore, the Dutch Art Council has prepared a list of criteria for galleries to conform to. One of the qualifications is that the galleries open at least four days a week. Also they must show a presentation-programme to prove their quality.

This class of commercial and other interesting galleries is listed below.

Most of the Amsterdam galleries specialise in post-War art, starting with the abstract-expressionist work of the international Cobra-group. Newly opened galleries present fresh-painted Dutch and international examples of the Trans-Avant-Garde. In between are galleries connected with artists from the generation in the years they were founded.

Therefore, only recently opened galleries seem to be interested in applications by unknown artists. Established galleries generally choose those who are talked about and fit into the collection. Studio-visits or house-calls are made, but seldom result in exhibitions.

But if you really are able to sustain a grim trip round the Amsterdam galleries, to show your work, please phone before you do and make sure you know (and appreciate) the style of the gallery you plan to visit. Young artists should try the alternative or artists' spaces listed in the next chapter.

Gallery applications are only welcomed when indicated in the following list.

Most established galleries are in the canal-zone near Leidsestraat and museum-area, new galleries can be found near the Jordaan-zone and the nearby canals.

Generally all galleries are closed on Sunday and Monday, and open from Tuesday-Saturday from 12-6.

All exhibitions of museums and galleries are monthly listed in the *"Amsterdamse Uitkrant"* published by the *Amsterdam Uit Buro, Leidseplein.* This Uitkrant is free, available at most museums, theatres, giro — and post offices, and from a box outside the Stadsschouwburg theatre between the American Hotel and the Leidseplein. Since March 1985 *ALERT* gallery diary F3.50 is on sale monthly for the current exhibition details.

At the end of March 400 Dutch major galleries organise a very large show of their collections in the Nieuwe Kerk on the Dam-square.

Amsterdam avant-garde galleries can be seen in June at RAI exhibition centre Europaplein at Amsterdam's International Art Fair.

MUSEUM AREA
Area south of Spui and Muntplein, with southern canal-zone between Leidsegracht and Amstel-river including Museum-quarter. *(Numbers refer to map.)*

Tram/bus stops are indicated by nearby street or square.

Galerie A, Kleine-Gartmanplantsoen 12, A'dam centrum. Telephone 227065. Tram 6, 7, 10; bus 26, 65, 66, 69 (Weteringschans/Leidseplein). *26*
Open Tue-Sat 2-6. Harry Ruhé's A gallery in the former Town Prison. Contemporary avant-garde art, specialisation: records, books by international artists.

Amazone, Keizersgracht 678, A'dam centrum. Telephone 279000. Tram 16, 24, 25 (Vijzelstraat). *5*
Open Tue-Fri 10-4, Saturday 1-4, Thursday-evening also from 7-9, closed Sundays. Activity centre for and by women with courses and projects in an exhibition-cellar. Shows with work by women-artists, various styles. Artists, however are chosen from the SVBK (Women Artists Foundation) archives.

Amro/street-gallery, Rembrandtsplein, A'dam centrum.
Tram 4, 9, 14. *11*
20th century Dutch art, day and night on view. Artists selected by Amro Kunstzaken, of Amro Bank.

Art & Project, Prinsengracht 785, A'dam centrum. Telephone 220372. Tram 16, 24, 25 (Vijzelstraat) or tram 6, 7, 10 (Weteringschans). *20*
Open Tue-Sat 1-5, Sundays and Mondays closed. One of Holland's

major galleries, located behind a black garage-door near the Nieuwe Spiegelstraat. Art & Project, founded in 1968, shows contemporary and avant-garde art, from the Netherlands or elsewhere in Europe. Paintings, (photo)sculptures, or installations, are arranged in the large exhibition spaces by the artists themselves. Among them: Barry Flanagan, Francesco Clemente, Nicolas Pope, Richard Long. From Holland many artists, who teach or studied at the Ateliers 63 in Haarlem, are presented: Ger van Elk, Toon Verhoef, Joris Geurts, Emo Verkerk, Ansuya Blom. Please, no applications!

Asselijn, Lange Leidsedwarsstraat 198-200, A'dam centrum. Telephone 249030. Tram 6, 7, 10, 16, 24, 25 (Weteringschans, Rijksmuseum). *27*
Open Tue-Sat 12-5. Gallery is located in the quarter near the Rijksmuseum. Contemporary Dutch graphics and drawings by Cassée, Plaat, Kracht, Gordijn, Oey, Vaassen, Roos, Woudstra. Mr. Bram Volkers is interested to look at new work, but admits it seldom leads to an exhibition.

Kunsthandel M. L. de Boer, Keizersgracht 542, A'dam centrum. Telephone 234060. Tram 1, 2, 5 (Leidsestraat). *18*
Open Tue-Sat 10-5. Traditional chic gallery in canal-house, dealing in 19th and 20th century realistic paintings, sculpture and graphics.

Brinkman, Kerkstraat 105, A'dam centrum. Telephone 227493. Tram 1, 2, 5 (Leidsestraat). *23*
Open Tue-Sat 12-6. Own choice of current art. Stocked are Schoonhoven, Engels and de Jong.

Canon Photo Gallery, Leidsestraat 79, A'dam centrum. Telephone 254494. Tram 1, 2, 5. *24*
Open Tue-Sat 11-6. Gallery, bookshop, showroom on modern photography. The photo-gallery also organises courses and special workshops. Photographers can leave their work for selection by Mr. Lorenzo Merlo and a special committee. They decide about possible exhibitions, each April and October. Contact: Mr. Lorenzo Merlo.

Collecton d'Art, Keizersgracht 516, A'dam centrum. Telephone 221511. Tram 1, 2, 5 (Leidsestraat) *17*
Open Tue-Sat 1-5. Another leading Amsterdam gallery, housed in a former book-shop, which was transformed in 1969 into this all white exhibition space, owned by Mrs. Cora de Vries. Post-war art, with specific interests: Cobra and abstract, expressionism: Appel, De Kooning, Van Velde, Armando. Realistic expressionism by Freymuth and Constant. Painting, sculpture and graphics.

Cricri, Alexander Boersstraat 4, A'dam zuid. Telephone 798401. Tram 2, 3, 5, 12, 16; bus 26, 65, 66, 67, 69 (Van Baerlestraat, Concertgebouw). *41*
Open Tue-Sat 12-5. Small relatively young gallery, right behind the Concertgebouw. Specialisation: graphics and drawings by young artists. Mrs. Jettie Albach is seriously interested in new small-sized work. Please apply by telephone, before showing your work.

Espace, Keizersgracht 548, A'dam centrum. Telephone 240802. Tram 1, 2, 5 (Leidsestraat). *19*
Open Tue-Sat 11-5.30. Since 1960 this canal-house gallery shows work

of the sixties and seventies: Cobra-artists Alechinsky, Corneille, Lucebert and New Figuration painting by Raveel, Lucassen. Also in stock are Breytenbach, Heyboer, Gubbels. Please, no applications.

Studio Evergreen, Prinsengracht 624, A'dam centrum. Telephone 257414. Tram 16, 24, 25 (Vijzelstraat). *32*
Garden-architects showing art related to gardens. Incidental shows. Contact Mr. Rietveld or Mr. v. d. Horst.

Gamma, Keizersgracht 429, A'dam centrum. Telephone 230767. Tram 1, 2, 5 (Leidsestraat). *16*
Open Tue-Sat 11.30-5.30. International painting, jewellery, graphics but further no specific fields. Owner is Mrs. R. Meulensteen. Gallery artists are: Co Westerik, Frank Lodeizen, Fon Klement, Sam Middleton.

Gooijer Fine Art, Prinsengracht 510, A'dam centrum. Telephone 245432. Tram 16, 24, 25 (Vijzelstraat). *25*
Open Tue-Sat 11-6. Various forms of modern expressionism, abstract painting and sculpture. Mr. Gooijer, who recently started this gallery, is interested in new work. Bring a well composed documentation and phone for application. Next to this a unique computer system registers names of interesting artists, showing in Holland as well as results of auctions etc. Artists are: Campi, Koener, Grassere and Gentry.

Guido de Spa, Tweede Weteringsdwarsstraat 34, A'dam centrum. Telephone 221528. Tram 6, 7, 10 (Weteringschans, Rijksmuseum). *35*
Open Wed-Sat 2-5. Simple home-gallery, expositions with ceramics, graphics, glass-works, paintings etc.

Heineken Galerij, Ferdinand Bolstraat, A'dam zuid. Tram 16, 24, 25. *2*
Open day and night. Open-air street gallery, sponsored by the brewery with the same name. Around the corner on the Stadhouderskade you can visit the Heineken Brewery itself. Generally amateur-artists exhibiting here. Contact Mr. Hesselius for applications: 138386/709111.

Hologrammen galerie, Prinsengracht 675, A'dam centrum. Telephone 229745. Tram 1, 2, 5 (Leidsestraat).
Showroom with interesting modern forms of tromp-l'oeil: three-dimensional, but flat, holographic laser-photos. The gallery is opened from Wed-Sun from 1.30-5, entrance f 3,- Holograms are also for sale.

Inart, Paulus Potterstraat 22, A'dam zuid. Telephone 641881. Tram 2, 3, 5, 12, 16; bus 26 (Van Baerlestraat, Stedelijk museum). *40*
Open Mon-Fri 9-5. Wholesale trading company with small gallery opposite the Stedelijk and Van Gogh Museums. Exhibitions with ceramics, glass-works, jewellery, painting and specialisation in Scandinavian and Dutch crafts. Bring photos and other documentation for application. Contact Mrs. Carla Koch.

Yaki Kornblit, Willemsparkweg 69, A'dam zuid. Telephone 628977. Tram 2. *42*
Open Tue-Sat 2-6. Kornblit introduced the American graffiti-artists Rimmelzee, Crash, Futura 2000, Dondi White, Quick, Blade, NOC 167, Blade and Zephyr in Europe. The graffiti elsewhere on walls in Amsterdam zuid has nothing to do with Mr. Yaki Kornblit's gallery, as his graffiti-artists now only paint or spray on canvas.

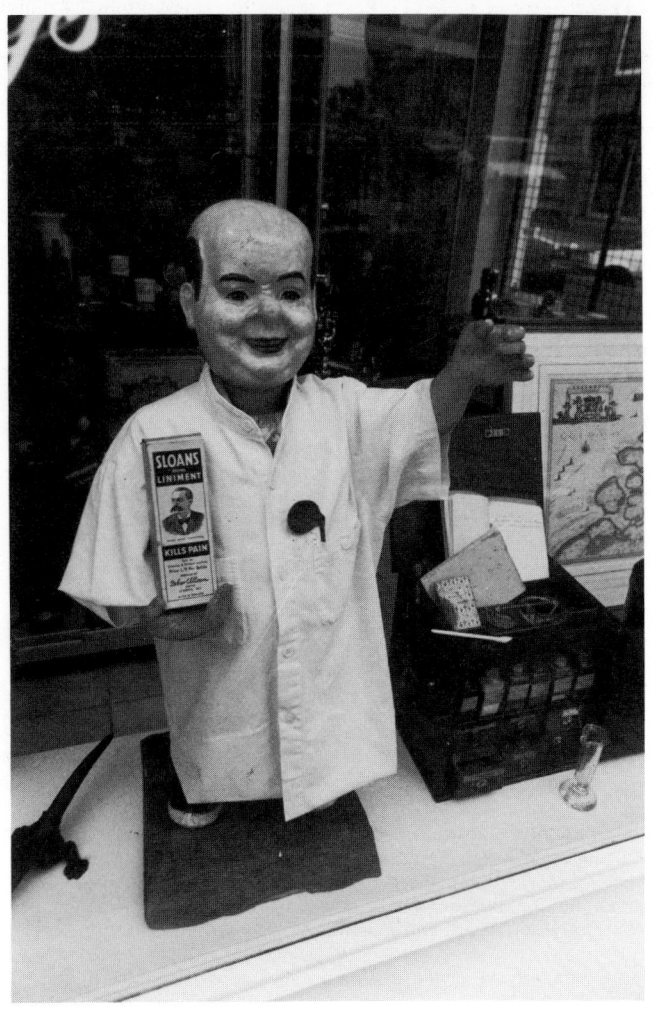

Medical antiquities and Dr Sloane himself on Prinsengracht

Lieve Hemel stoot je hoofd niet, Vijzelstraat 6-8, A'dam centrum. Telephone 230060. Tram 16, 24, 25. *34*
Open Tue-Sat 12-6. Thursday only from 12-2. "Good heavens, don't hurt your head", the translation of the odd name of the gallery indicates its location in a low cellar. Since 1968 Lieve Hemel presents contemporary fine-painted realism. Paintings, ceramics, graphics made by strictly Dutch artists Van Brussel, Voorzaat, Kanters.

Nieuw Perspektief, Amstel 34, A'dam centrum. Telephone 263952. Tram 4, 9, 14, 16, 24, 25 (Muntplein). *12*
Open Tue-Fri 10-6 and Saturday 1-6. Idealistic contemporary art and cul-

ture centre set up by Mr. Pieter Kooiman, founder of the SBK Art-hire elsewhere in the city. This foundation however doesn't rent art but organises exhibitions with arts and crafts: painting, sculpture, ceramic, jewellery, photograph. Incidental "coffee-concerts" on Sunday mornings. Only group shows of artists are organised; the work is kept on consignment. Amsterdam-based artists can apply.

Polychrome, Frans Halsstraat 9, A'dam zuid. Telephone 794745. Tram 16, 24, 25 (Stadhouderskade/F. Bolstraat). *1*
Open Tue-Sat 1-6. Printmakers workshop, as well as regular shows of editions of prints made here by current artists Cremer, Paolozzi, Lataster, Raveel, Constant, Gubbels, Dumas, Visch. (see: Workshops)

Print Galerij Pieter Brattinga, Prinsengracht 628, A'dam centrum. Telephone 224265. Tram 16, 24, 25 (Vijzelstraat). *33*
Open Mon-Fri 11-4. Printer/Print-gallery showing contemporary graphics by mainly Dutch artists. Brattinga is located opposite the Printshop, mentioned below. (see also: Workshops)

Printshop, Prinsengracht 845, A'dam centrum. Telephone 251656. Tram 16, 24, 25 (Vijzelstraat). *29*
Open Mon-Sat 10-1 and 2-5.30. Master printer Piet Clement shows contemporary international graphics, printed in his large workshop, but also paintings and drawings made by the same artists. Some years ago David Hockney's "Six Fairy Tales" were printed and shown here. Large stock containing work by: Raveel, Lodeizen, Voet, Mutsaers, Lataster, Constant. (see also: Workshops)

Ra, Vijzelstraat 80, A'dam centrum. Telephone 265100. Tram 16, 24, 25. *31*
Open Tue-Fri 12-6, Saturday 11-5. Unique international collection of experimental jewellery. The gallery is placed in the belly of the large ABN bank building. During the early seventies Dutch jewellery artists such as Emmy van Leersum started working with simple and cheap materials, making way for a revolutionary form of this craft. Nowadays Paul Derrez of Ra edits his own publications and sells interesting catalogues. In stock: Herbst, Lam de Wolf, Laken, Boekhoudt, Derrez.

Rob Art, Weteringschans 273, A'dam centrum. Telephone 254686. Tram 6, 7, 10 or tram 3, 4 (Frederiksplein). *4*
Rob combines a very specialised leather-shop with another special interest: the art of the homo-erotic scene. Among his art is a certain Mister Tom of Finland. Applications are always welcome, just ask for Rob!

Van Rooy, Nieuwe Spiegelstraat 43, A'dam centrum. Telephone 229621. Tram 6, 7, 10 (Weteringschans, Rijksmuseum). *21*
Open Tue-Sat 1-5. Modern architecture and other recent developments on design. Show of sketches, screen-prints. Stocked architects are Berlage and Rem Koolhaas.

Srefidensi, Keizersgracht 757, A'dam centrum. Telephone 223725. Tram 4 (Utrechtsestraat). *9*
Open daily 10-5. Cultural exhibition centre of work, made by artists from the Caribbean Islands, the West Indies and Surinam. No applications because they have a very busy programme.

SBK galerij, Vijzelstraat opposite 80, A'dam centrum. Telephone c/o SBK 239215. Tram 16, 24, 25. *30.*
Open day and night. Street gallery, covered by ABN bank, presenting a monthly choice of work from the SBK Art-hire collection. (see also: Art-hire)

STOV, Lange Leidsedwarsstraat 208, A'dam centrum. Telephone 230967. Tram 6, 7, 10 (Weteringschans, Rijksmuseum). *28*
Open Mon 1-5.30, Tue-Fri 10.30-5.30, Sat 11-4. STOV, a centre for textile art and education, organises exhibitions of contemporary textile art, courses and lectures. Information and specialised books and magazines for public inspection.

Swart, Van Breestraat 23, A'dam zuid. Telephone 764736. Tram 3, 5, 12; bus 26 (Van Baerlestraat, Concertgebouw) *43*
Open Tue-Sat 2-6. Important gallery, situated in a quite street behind the Concertgebouw. Mrs. Riekje Swart recently introduced the French "Figuration Libre" in Holland after years of specialization in abstract art. Now there are also new Dutch avant-garde painters, video-artists, and sculptors. Represented artists: van 't Slot, Struycken (video), Combas, van der Haak, Mosselman and others.

Tribe, Weteringschans 165, A'dam centrum. Tram 6, 7, 10. *3*
Open Wed-Sat 2-6. Temporary art space in empty office-hall near tram-stop next to the Weteringplantsoen. Sometimes some reasonable art is on show here.

Wetering, Lijnbaansgracht 288/Spiegelgracht, A'dam centrum. Telephone 236189. Tram 6, 7, 10 (Weteringschans, Rijksmuseum). *36*
Open Tue-Sat 12-5. No specific line, but fine personal choice of contemporary Dutch painting, sculpture, graphics etc. Among Wetering-artists are: Stoop, De Vaal, Van der Pol, Knoote, Schierbeek, Bragdon. Manager/owner of the gallery is Mr. Michiel Hennus.

De Witte Voet, Kerkstraat 149, A'dam centrum. Telephone 258412. Tram 1, 2, 5 (Leidsestraat). *22*
Open Tue-Sat 12-5. One of the leading current arts and crafts galleries of Amsterdam. Double-exhibitions with special interest in modern ceramics. Mrs. Annemie Boissevains stocks the work of Flor, Hahn, Moonen, Oestereicher and Lichtveld.

Stichting Wonen, Leidsestraat 5, A'dam centrum. Telephone 230984. Tram 1, 2, 5. *15*
Strictly no commercial gallery but documentary centre with exhibitions about urbanisation and architecture.

Zuid, Johannes Verhulststraat 101, A'dam zuid. Telephone 625664. Tram 16 (De Lairessestraat). *44*
Open Tue-Sat 1-5. Artist-operated gallery of Mr. Peter Bakker selecting his fellow-artists for exhibition. Interested in current graphics, drawings and paintings between abstract and figurative.

JORDAAN AREA
Area west of Dam-square and Muntplein, with western canal-zone between Haarlemmerstraat and Leidsegracht including the Jordaan-quarter. *(Numbers refer to the map.)*

Trams/bus stops are indicated by nearby street.

Paul Andriesse, Prinsengracht 116, A'dam centrum. Telephone 236237. Tram 13, 14, 17; bus 21, 67 (Rozengracht/Westermarkt). *16*
Open Tue-Sat 2-6. Leading gallery showing avant-garde painting, sculpture, mixed media by Höckelmann, Gudmundsun, Izaks, Daniëls, Andriesse, Marlene Dumas. Paul Andriesse's gallery was known before as Galerie Helen van der Mey.

Annex galerie, Tweede Rozendwarsstraat 3A, A'dam centrum (Jordaan). Telephone 272209. Tram 13, 14, 17; bus 21, 67 (Rozengracht). *9*
Open Wed-Sat 2-6. Young home-gallery in a recently built part of the Jordaan presenting new forms of painting and installations by young artists. The gallery is connected with an actor's studio. Contact Hans Bant.

Arti et Amicitae, Rokin 112, A'dam centrum. Telephone 233508. Tram 4, 9, 14, 16, 24, 25 (Muntplein). *37*
Open Mon-Sat 12-5. Highly scenic, early 19th century exhibition space belonging to the artists-union with private-restaurant and café for its members. Nearby the impressive stairs are names of famous Dutch impressionists Breitner, Israels and Maks are preserved for eternity. Arti organizes its own "group-salons" in spring and autumn, but also photo, fashion, crafts-exhibitions.

Arti galerie, Spui la, A'dam centrum. Telephone 233508. Tram see above. *36.*
Open Tue-Fri 12-6, Saturday 12-5. Just around the corner from Arti, small gallery belonging to society with double shows by individual members. It is possible to organize your own exhibitions here.

Bedaux, Nieuwe Leliestraat 96, A'dam centrum (Jordaan). Telephone 228294. Tram 13, 14, 17 (Westermarkt). *13*
Open day and night. Street-window gallery. Phone for further information.

Binnen, Egelantiersgracht 31, A'dam centrum (Jordaan). Telephone 259603. Tram 13, 14, 17; bus 21, 67 (Westermarkt). *15*
Open Tue-Fri 12-6, Saturday 11-5. Exhibition space connected with the workshop of two young interior-architects Anne Lawant and Helen van Ruiten. They show work by colleagues, but also sometimes art or toy exhibitions. Willing to look at work.

d'Eendt, Spuistraat 272/Raamsteeg 2, A'dam centrum. Telephone 266577/243064. Tram 1, 2, 5, 13, 17 (N. Z. Voorburgwal/Spui). *28*
Open Tue-Sat 10-6. International gallery, one of the oldest in Amsterdam. Ethnographics and contemporary international — and 19th century — paintings, ceramics, graphics, drawings. Gallery artists: Kitaj, Picasso, Chagall, Archipenko, Hockney, Pascin, Schröder-Sonnestern (psychopathic artist), Wutruba, De Vlaminck, Melle and others.

Etcetera, Spuistraat 72, A'dam centrum. Telephone 251136. Tram 1, 2, 5 (Spui). *46*
Artist-operated exhibition-space, Etcetera is Hans Frisch' home-gallerys. Frisch's other gallery is **Kreatorium,** Ceintuurbaan 426-430, A'dam Zuid, tram 16, 24, 25. Shows with contemporary paintings, video, collages, installations, performances etc. Kreatorium is open from Thu-Sat 12-6 and by appointment, Etcetera is only open by appointment.

Barbara Farber, Herengracht 340, A'dam centrum. Telephone 276343. Tram 1, 2, 5 (Spui/Koningsplein). *24*
Open Tue-Sat 12-5.30. American graffiti and other new forms of American and European avant-garde art. Interesting exhibitions. Gallery artists: Salle, Haring, Oldenburg, Dink, Kohlhofer, Warhol, Christo. All artists are selected, mainly in the United States by Jules & Barbara Farber themselves. Not open to applications.

Jules Farber of Barbara Farber gallery, Herengracht

Hans Gieles, Spuistraat 3, A'dam centrum. Telephone 237292. Tram/bus: walk from Central Station westwards direction Haarlemmerstraat. *52*
Open Tue-Sun 12-6. Young, recently opened, small-sized gallery, overlooking the Sonesta Hotel at the Kattengat. Shows generally young and

Hans Gieles, gallerist, during exhibition of Peter Verhaar

promising artists from Holland, and in the near future also from elsewhere. Among Gieles artists are Verhaar, Studulski and Domburg. Before starting his own gallery Hans Gieles was an assistant at the above mentioned Farber gallery.

Den Gulden Fonteyn, Singel 166, A'dam centrum. Telephone 243151. Tram 1, 2, 5, 13, 17 (N. Z. Voorburgwal, Royal Palace). *47*
Open 12-5. No specific field, realistic painting, various forms of ceramics, drawings etc. Also open by appointment.

Hamer, Leliegracht 38, A'dam centrum (Jordaan). Telephone 267394. Tram 13, 14, 17 (Westermarkt). *18*
Open Tue-Sat 1-6.30. Leading gallery of naive art from Holland, Yugoslavia, Caribbean, France, England etc. Applications by naive artists are welcomed by Mr. Nico van der Endt.

Staircase in Hans Gieles' gallery, Spuistraat

Jurka, Singel 28, A'dam centrum. Telephone 266733. Tram/bus/metro: walk from Central Station, direction Haarlemmerstraat, west of the station. *53*
Open Wed-Sun 12-5. Trend-setting gallery, presenting very current forms of international painting, sculpture and photography. Jurka also sells some books, magazines and catalogues. Portfolios are also sold. Klashorst, Ploeg, Bach, Haka, de Beus, Nobbe, Robert Mapplethorpe, Andrea are presented by owner Rob Jurka.

Krikhaar, Spuistraat 330, A'dam centrum. Telephone 267166. Tram 1, 2, 5 (Spui). *27*
Open Tue-Sat 10.30-6. Twenty-year old gallery with Cobra and expressionists in stock. Among the famous artists represented here are Alechinsky, Appel, Corneille, Jorn, Rooskens, Wolvecamp, Miro, Picasso, Chagall (paintings, drawings, gouaches, graphics). Mr. Krikhaar plans a year in advance, but he is willing to look at work and gives advice if necessary.

Van Krimpen, Prinsengracht 629, A'dam centrum. Telephone 229375. Tram 1, 2, 5 (Spui). *1*
Open Tue-Sat 2-6. Avant-garde painting from Holland and Germany by Disler, Piet Dieleman, Förg, Rob van Koningsbruggen. Gallery is next to the public library and **"Art Book", an art book-shop.**

Lageman, Prinsengracht 260, A'dam centrum. Telephone 220695. Tram 13, 14, 17 (Westermarkt). *5*
Open Tue-Sat 11-5. Mr. Gerard Lageman, sculptor himself, is interested in looking at your work, but only if you are from somewhere in Europe and make graphics, paintings or sculptures, fitting into his figurative-oriented collection. Also ceramics and small bronzes, which like all artworks here, never cost over D fl. 500.

The Living Room, Laurierstraat 70, A'dam centrum (Jordaan). Telephone 258449. Tram 13, 14, 17 (Westermarkt). *8*
Open Tue-Sat 2-6. Bart van der Ven's gallery, which moved from his living-room to a real exhibition-space is in a narrow Jordaan street. New developments by young Dutch artists, sometimes very interesting shows of paintings, sculptures, installations, etc. Among artists are: Sanders, Veneman, van Vreden, van den Broek and the — recently split-up — artists-duo Mantje & Vlugt.

Lughien, Reestraat 17, A'dam centrum. Telephone 253193. Tram 13, 14, 17 (Westermarkt). *22*
Open Tuesday and Thursday from 11-5, Friday and Saturday 11-5.30. Across the Prinsengracht. Small gallery presenting figurative graphics and ceramics.

Merlo, Reestraat 19, A'dam centrum. Telephone 256461. Tram 13, 14, 17 (Westermarkt). *21.*
Open Wed-Sat 1-6. Next to Lughien, presenting similar young Dutch developments in figurative painting, ceramics and graphics. Professional artists can try to apply to Mrs. Marijke Merlo.

Mokum, Oude Zijds Voorburgwal 334, A'dam centrum. Telephone 243958. Tram 4, 9, 14, 16, 24, 25 (Muntplein). *39*
Open Tue-Sat 11-6. Mokum, nickname of Amsterdam, shows Dutch friendly surrealistic paintings by various artists.

Nieuwezijds, Nieuwe Zijds Voorburgwal 306, A'dam centrum. Telephone 226751. Tram 1, 2, 5, 13, 17 (N. Z. Voorburgwal, post office). *30*
Open Tue-Sat 11-5. Jenke Kaldenberg, classical pianist by profession, claims his gallery to be non-commercial and non-specialist. A friendly atmosphere is guaranteed.

Olympus, Herengracht 86, A'dam centrum. Telephone 240084. Tram 1, 2, 5, 13, 17 (N. Z. Voorburgwal). *50*
Open Tue-Sat 2-5. International orientated photography-gallery, out of four in Amsterdam. Also exchange-exhibitions with photo-galleries abroad. Regular shows of new forms of photography; for example the staged photo-events by Bernard Faucon. Mr. Ger Fiolet, owner of Olympus, is open to applications, but strictly by appointment.

Paladijn, Singel 26, A'dam centrum. Telephone 220865. Tram/bus/metro: walk westwards of Central Station, direction Haarlemmerstraat *54.*
Open Wed-Sun 12-5. Neighbour gallery of Jurka, although Mr. Dick de Bruin's artistic manifestations take place in a cellar. New tendencies in painting, photographs, video. Among these video-artists are Lydia Schouten and Elsa Standsfield/Madelon Hooykaas.

Petit, Nieuwe Zijds Voorburgwal 270, A'dam centrum. Telephone 267507. Tram 1, 2, 5 (Royal Palace). *33*
Open Tue-Sat 12-6. Once really a small gallery, now an exhibition space with two floors, presenting lyrical, realistic drawings, etchings, paintings, sculpture. Among Petit artists are Wijnberg, van Poppel, Donker, Kuik, Vos, van Rossum, Stam, Homan, Eyzenbach and van Kruiningen. Walking in the cellar, mind your head if you are over six feet — nearly 2 meters — long. Mr. Tom van Dijk welcomes applications, but only if the works fit into his collection. Petit organised together with d'Eendt and De Witte Voet the most recent gallery-presentation in the Nieuwe Kerk. Petit is next to the Sothmann gallery behind the Stamp-market.

Plein 7, da Costaplein 7, A'dam west. Telephone 183368. Tram 13, 14 (de Clerqstraat).
Open Mon-Fri 10-5, Saturday 1-6. Small gallery presenting arts and crafts.

Rozengalerij, Rozengracht 75, A'dam centrum. Telephone 221990. Tram 13, 14, 17. *12*
Open Tue-Fri 1.30-6, Saturday 11-5. Glass works, unica, jewellery made out of glass or perspex. Also graphics by international artists.

Kunsthandel Siau, Keizersgracht 267, A'dam centrum. Telephone 267621. Tram 1, 2, 5, 13, 17 (N. Z. Voorburgwal/Dam). *23*
Open Tue-Sat 10-5, Sundays 2-5. Also secretariat of Dutch Union of Contemporary Art Dealers and Galleries. Mr. Siau's personal choice of contemporary figurative arts. Artists include: Boin, Deckwitz, Lipton.

Sothmann, Nieuwe Zijds Voorburgwal 284, A'dam centrum. Telephone 236920. Tram 1, 2, 5 (post office). *31*
Open Tue-Sat 12-5. Recently re-opened 20th century art gallery. (see: Antique/art dealers)

Steltman, Westermarkt 27, A'dam centrum (Jordaan). Telephone 228683. Tram 13, 14, 17. *20*
Open Tue-Sat 11-6. International figurative arts and crafts.

Interior of SBK art hire centre, N.Z. Voorburgwal

La Strada, Elandsgracht 12, A'dam centrum (Jordaan). Telephone 265249. Tram 7, 10 (Marnixstraat, police office). *4*
Open Tue-Sat 2-6. Recently opened gallery in front of an architects work-room. Mrs. Eliane Nagelkerke plans to present young artists here.

SBK, N. Z. Voorburgwal 325, A'dam centrum. Telephone 239215. Tram 1, 2, 5. *29*
Open Tue-Sat 10-5. Small exhibition-space next to the halls where the art-hire collection is shown to the members of the SBK(Foundation Visual Arts). **SBK-street gallery:** Vijzelstraat. (see also: Art hire)

d'Theeboom, Singel 210, A'dam centrum. Telephone 237299. Tram 1, 2, 5, 13, 17 (N. Z. Voorburgwal, post office). *48*
Open Mon-Sat 1-5.30. Housed in an old canal house carrying this name (tea-tree) which also contains a hi-tech coffee-shop/tea-room. Interesting Dutch and foreign artists show their paintings, pastels, and sculpture: Hans v.d. Ban, Branka Perosevic, Mon Wolters.

Torch, Prinsengracht 218, A'dam centrum. Telephone 260284. Tram 13, 17 (Westermarkt). *6.* Director: Mr. Adrian v. d. Have.
Open Tue-Sat 12-6. Brand new, contemporary photography with promising first exhibition.

$2\frac{1}{2} \times 4\frac{1}{2}$, Looiersgracht 1, A'dam centrum. Telephone 279635. Tram 7, 10 (Marnistraat, police office). *2*
Open Saturday 1-6. Well, another brand-new photography gallery, but still too early to say something about specializations and quality.

Vassalucci, Singel 38 A'dam centrum. Telephone: 230270.
Open Thu-Sun 12-5. Contemporary art, new exhibition space.
Director: Michel Vassalucci.

Nanky de Vreeze, Singel 37, A'dam centrum. Telephone 273808. Tram/bus/metro: walk from Central Station direction Sonesta Hotel. *51*

Glass-works in gallery Nanky de Vreeze, Singel

Open Tue-Fri 11-6, Saturday 11-5. Contemporary painting, sculptures, ceramics with interesting specialization in glass-works. Please, no applications!

Wave galleries, Nieuwe Leliestraat 81, A'dam centrum (Jordaan). Telephone 265577. Tram 13, 14, 17 (Westermarkt). *17*
Open Tue-Fri 12-6, Saturday 12-5. Modern realism, sometimes also color-copy art shows.

Fons Welters, Palmdwarstraat 36, A'dam central (Jordaan). Telephone: 227193.
Open Tues-Sat 2-6. New exhibition space. Director: Mr. Fons Welters. Specialists in modern sculpture and installations.

Other parts of Amsterdam

Maghi Bettini, Warmoesstraat 16A, A'dam centrum. Telephone 224301. Tram/bus/metro: walk direction St. Nicolaas Kerk, east of the Central Station.
Open Wed-Sat 1-5.30. No specific style but more personal choice of international ceramics and painting.

Cone 3, Van Ostadestraat 152, A'dam zuid. Telephone 733292. Tram 3, 12, 16, 24, 25 (Ceintuurbaan).
Open Wednesday and Saturday 11-5, Thursday and Friday 11-4. New ceramics gallery, founded by enthusiastic ceramic artists who are willing to help you look for a work-shop or give lessons in ceramics. Next to all that, also interested in new artists who like to exhibit their art, preferably graphics and painting. Shows of generally abstract ceramics and graphics.

Liesbeth Lips, Recht Boomssloot 26, A'dam centrum. Telephone: 250235. Metro: Nieuwmarkt.
Open Wed-Sat 12-5. Mrs Lips, the director, has taken over Sponz's artist space (see cover photo). Contemporary sculpture, painting and drawing.

Other books and so, 10 Katestraat 53, A'dam west. Telephone 121233. Tram 7, 17 (Kinkerstraat).
Ulysses Carrión shows his highly interesting collection of artists-books only by appointment.

Religie-gallery, Oudekerksplein 23, A'dam centrum. Telephone 223931. Metro Nieuwmarkt.
Open Mon-Sat 10-4. The only specialization the Amsterdam galleries missed finally filled up — religion; situated between the sins of the nearby red light district and the strict faith embodied by the beautiful Oude Kerk (Old Church). Regular shows of icons and religious paintings and drawings.

Lambert Tegenbosch, Nassaukade 126, A'dam west. Telephone 842507. Bus 21 (Hugo de Grootplein) or tram 13, 14 (de Clerqstraat).
Open Tue-Sat 2-6 and by appointment. Early 20th century art. Paintings, graphics, sculptures, drawings by Paul Klee, Edvard Munch, Kees Verwey, Rik Wouters, James Ensor, Pierre Alechinsky, Pablo Picasso.

Exposorium Vrije Universiteit, De Boelelaan 1105, A'dam Buitenveldert. Bus 23-26.
Open Mon-Fri 10-8. Free University Display room. Different contemporary art forms, sometimes already exhibited elsewhere in the city. Contact Mr. Frieze.

Wending, Rubensstraat 60, A'dam zuid. Telephone 718630, by appointment only. Tram 24 (Stadionweg).
Permanent collection covering 1900-60, and including paintings and graphics by Karel Appel, Kees Maks, Harmen Meurs and Loe Loeber.

ART HIRE

In Amsterdam both **Artotheek** and **SBK (Foundation Visual Arts)** hire art. Paintings, sculptures, photographs, textiles, graphics, glass-works, ceramics — unfortunately no video-tapes yet — made by contemporary Amsterdam based artists.

The origin of the collections makes the difference. Cheapest way to rent art is the **Artotheek,** where the work is selected by the BKB (State Aid) and Artotheek-committee board. In exchange for a salary and financial compensation for artistic expenses, artists handed in their work to the State, who "bought" it. Therefore the Artotheek-works cannot be purchased anymore by its members.

SBK buys or rent work, they select every year from a public entry among Dutch-based professional artists. Members of SBK save a part of their rent for a future art purchase out of the SBK collection. All three hire-centres have small exhibition-centres:

Artotheek Noord, Papaverweg 5B, A'dam noord. Telephone 321336. Bus 35, 36, 37 (Klaprozenweg).

Artotheek Osdorp, De Meervaart, Osdorpplein 67, A'dam Osdorp. Telephone 196945. Tram 1; bus 19, 23.
Both open Tuesday 1-6, 7-9, Wednesday and Friday 1-6, Saturday 11-4.

Artotheek art hire centre 'De Meervaart', Osdorpplein, Amsterdam Osdorp

Artotheek Oost, Derde Oosterparkstraat 201, A'dam oost. Telephone 681753. Tram 3.
Open Tuesday and Wednesday 2-9, Friday and Saturday 12-5.

SBK, kunstuitleencentrum, N. Z. Voorburgwal 325, A'dam centrum. Tram 1, 2, 5.
Open Tue-Fri 10-5, Saturday 9-5. (see also: Commercial galleries)

ART GROUPS AND THEIR EXHIBITION SPACES

Discontented with the traditional, commercial galleries young artists started their own exhibition-spaces, where also (unsaleable) performances and installations are held. Most buildings, former warehouses in the city or in the harbour are hired or squatted and afterwards with municipal authorities approval used temporarily by artists. Some art-spaces are opened as work-shops for foreign colleagues as well. Showing or working there means you have to make a financial investment, smaller than in commercial galleries. The combination dealer/artist, although is sometimes difficult to sustain, so many "alternative" art spaces close down, after two years or more.

Visiting the art-spaces you are confronted with surprising, frightening, or incomprehensible-forms of art by young artists. In most cases you can discuss the work with the artist, who is present at his or her own exhibition.

Because of the unpredictable politics of most art-groups it's advisable to call before visit, inquiring whether the spaces are still open. *(Numbers refer to the map.)*

Aorta, Spuistraat 189, A'dam centrum. Telephone 271287. Tram 1, 2, 5, 13, 17 (Dam, N. Z. Voorburgwal). *32*
Open Tue-Sat 12-6. The enormous space is used as a workshop and exhibition-room. In a small gallery upstairs one-man shows are held. Aorta was founded in 1982 by two young and one more experienced artists. They chose the former press-hall of a deserted newspaper building, nowadays inhabited by many young people. As one of the leading "alternative-galleries" the artists of Aorta have to cope with many exhibition-requests by colleagues, which generally cannot be granted anymore. Last season Aorta had exchange shows with groups from Berlin and Düsseldorf, showing paintings and sculpture. Contact for further information: Sonja Oudendijk or Bart Domburg.

Bolshuis, Rozengracht 105, A'dam centrum (Jordaan). Telephone 266328. Tram 13, 14 17. *11*
Open Mon-Fri 10-1, Wednesday 10-5. Former "genever" (gin) factory-building now housing several Jordaan artists who show here.

Atelier 408, Herengracht 408, A'dam centrum. Telephone 229314. Tram 1, 2, 5 Leidsestraat. *14*
Open Tue-Sat 12-6. Cellar gallery, where young artists show and promote their work. No specific line or art-group involved. The attractive space is owned by architect Mr. J. van Stigt, who informs you about the possibilities to show here.

05'T is the name of an art-group, that used to have its own exhibition-space as well. Now they are planning staged events, installations created on the spot, in combination with theatre, poetry, music elsewhere in the country or city. Henk Lotsy is willing to tell you about current activities of 05'T. Telephone 921228.

De Schottenburch, Krom Boomssloot 18, A'dam centrum. Telephone 947173/256171. Metro (Nieuwmarkt).
Open Wed-Sat 12-5. Artist/dealer/teacher Wim Vonk hand-restored his warehouse overlooking a tiny canal in the Nieuwmarkt area. Schottenburch is both for exhibitions and studio. Installations and thematic exhibitions by Amsterdam and sometimes Greenlandish artists.

Former press hall now studio and exhibition space of Aorta, Spuistraat

De Schottenburch's Wim Vonk with visitors in his gallery

De Selby, Hoptille 178, Amsterdam Bullewijk. Telephone 960064. Metro (Bullewijk/northern exit).
De Selby, strictly no gallery, is without a doubt the world's smallest exhibition space, housed in the room of artist Jan Gehlens studio/house in the new built Bullewijk area. Gehlen invites colleagues for his day-lit exhibitions with avant-garde painting, sculpture and installations. De Selby is opened, according to the day-light, in summertime generally on Friday, Saturday and Sunday from 2-5.

Montevideo, Buiksloterweg 5, A'dam noord. Telephone 237101. Tram/bus: take the ferry right behind the Central Station, cross the IJ harbour. Montevideo is the first building on your left after leaving the boat. *58.* Open every Thursday-evening at 8.15 and by appointment. Admission f 2,50, with CJP reduction f 1,50. Major centre of video-art: production, documentation, distribution of foreign video-art. Every Thursday evening sessions with video. Montevideo helps you also making your own-artistic-video production (see: Workshops and materials) and rents equipment. Contact: Mr. René Coelho.

NL Centrum, Rozengracht 168, A'dam centrum (Jordaan). Telephone 258477. Tram 13, 14, 17. *10*
Open daily 10-6. Centre, where artists can exchange thoughts and ideas, sometimes resulting in debates. Publication of leaflets, musical events.

Grafisch collectief Thoets, Nassaukade 321, A'dam west. Telephone 183543. Tram 7, 17 (Kinkerstraat).
Open Tue-Sat 1-6. Graphic artists' co-op, work-shop and exhibition-room, there are sometimes possibilities to rent this workshop. Phone for information, ask Mr. Jan Baas or one of his fellow graphic artists.

Oey's etalage, Prinsengracht 128, A'dam centrum. Telephone 249097. Tram 13, 14, 17 (Rozengracht).
Open night and day. Installations and objects exhibited by artist and pharmacist in his former shop.

Lumen Travo, Nieuwe Zijds Voorburgwal 352 IV, A'dam centrum. Telephone 278049/277435. Tram 1, 2, 5 (Spui). *26*
Open Tue-Sat 2-6, but irregular exhibitions. Owner Marian van Tilborg wants her home-gallery to be a salon, where artists make their début. She is interested to look at different kinds of work, but lets her own preferences take precedence. The gallery is located four floors above the Athenaeum Bookshop, employer of the dealer. Lumen Travo offers you as well as the joy of looking at art, a splendid aerial view of the Spui.

Makkom, Haarlemmerstraat 39, A'dam centrum. Telephone 277495. Tram: walk from Central Station. *56*
Open Tue-Sat 2-6. Organisation of artists with special interest in performance, theatre and artist-workshops. Makkom, a name derived from the Hebrew "place", edits its own magazine. The people of Makkom are especially interested in a more intellectual approach to art: Individual process-like exhibitions as well as international exchanges. Contact Mr. Josef Beman.

Centrum voor Vrouwen in de Beeldende Kunst, Zoutkeetsgracht 118. Telephone 248456. Tram 3 (terminal).
Open Thursday, Friday and Saturday 1-5. Women-artists centre with special workshops, performances, installations and exhibitions. Phone for information.

Stichting Edelweis, Levantkade 12, A'dam noord. Telephone 259971. Bus 28.
Studios in a former warehouse overlooking the IJ harbour. No studios however available, only in some cases for special projects. Primarily female artists work here, exhibiting each September. Contact Leonie Greefkens or Thérèse van Gelder.

Het Februari Collectief, Rozenstraat 5, A'dam centrum (Jordaan). Tram 13, 14, 17 (Rozengracht). *7*
When shows are held: open Sat-Sun 1-5, Tuesday 10-4. Artists-co-op, dealing with political mural paintings, like those on the Mozes en Aäronkerk near the Waterlooplein. Anti-fascism and anti-racism manifestations.

Taller, Keizersgracht 607, A'dam centrum. Telephone 246734. Tram 16, 24, 25 (Vijzelstraat). *7*
Open Wed-Sat 11-5, Sundays 1-5. Multi-media centre for South-American artists, showing their own work and theatre production. Also a coffee-shop. Next to Museum Fodor.

Visible voice, Oude Zijds Voorburgwal 160, A'dam centrum. Telephone 262866. Tram/bus/metro: walk from Central Station, direction St. Nicolaas Church. *41*
Open daily 4-10, or by appointment. Various art-forms.

Warmoesstraat 139, Warmoesstraat 139, A'dam centrum. No telephone connection. Tram 1, 2, 4, 5, 16, 24, 25 (Dam). *43*
Once one of the most active alternative galleries in the city now the Warmoesstraat has promoted itself to a museum. Every Thursday afternoon you can buy or exchange work in this Museum (paintings, books etc), directed by Mr. Ad de Jong.

FOREIGN CULTURAL CENTRES

Except for the Flemish cultural centre, of course, all Amsterdam-based foreign cultural centres organise language and culture-courses. Other activities include conferences, films, video, concerts. Each centre lends books and/or records. Generally foreign artists living in Holland show their artistic or literary work in the exhibition-spaces. The American Library was unfortunately closed down some years ago.

The British Council, Keizersgracht 343, A'dam centrum. Telephone 223644. Tram 1, 2, 5 (Leidsestraat/Koningsplein).
Open Mon-Fri 9-5, closed between 1-1.45, Fridays open from 9-4.45. A place to find British newspapers in the library. Information services, specialized language-courses, literature-lectures, scholarships. The British Council has promoted for over 50 years the values, the language and culture of Britain overseas. No official exhibition space.

Centrum voor Chileense Cultuur, Nieuwe Herengracht 29, A'dam centrum. Telephone 265258. Tram 7, 10 (Waterlooplein).
Open Mon-Fri 1-5. Non-official, because it is the cultural centre of Chilean artists in resistance. Shows of political work.

Maison Descartes, Vijzelgracht 2A, A'dam centrum. Telephone 224936. Tram 16, 24, 25.
Open Mon-Fri. 10-6. The French cultural centre, placed next to the Embassy, uses the beautiful 17th century building, where French philosopher René Descartes lived, preferring the Dutch liberal state of mind in those days. Also language-courses, library, discotheque, tele-club and interesting lectures. Last spring Emmanuel Le Roy Ladurie explained his book "Montaillou" to a polite French speaking Amsterdam audience.

Public library of the British Council, Herengracht

French cultural centre, Maison Descartes, Vijzelgracht

Goethe Institut, Herengracht 470, A'dam centrum. Telephone 230421. Tram 16, 24, 25 (Vijzelstraat).
Open Mon-Fri 11-6. Enthusiastic West German cultural center in a pleasant canal house. Language courses, library, film club, interesting (literary) expositions about "Exil" writers, Kafka etc.

Istituto Italiano di Cultura per I paessi Bassi, Keizersgracht 564, A'dam centrum. Telephone 265314. Tram 1, 2, 5 (Leidsestraat).
Open on week-days 9-6. Small shows with work by Italians in residence. 'Cinema, concerts, to hear your favourite Vivaldi or watch a Fellini-movie. Entrance-fees.

Vlaams Cultureel Centrum, Nes 45, A'dam centrum. Telephone 229014. Tram 4, 16, 24, 25 (Rokin).
Includes De Brakke Grond Theatre. Exhibitions of Belgian art. This large Flemish Cultural Center replaces a drive down to Ghent or Brussels to enjoy Belgian first class theatre. The Brakke Grond is shared by Dutch and Belgian companies. Also good modern café.

PLACES OF ARCHITECTURAL INTEREST

Already during the 17th century Amsterdam citizens proudly claimed their city owned the eighth world-wonder: their Townhall built by Jacob van Campen, nowadays used as a Royal Palace.

Next to this architectural "wonder" and the unmistaken beauty of the canal-houses, the Amsterdam municipality developed more interesting town-planning projects.

At the beginning of this century, the Amsterdam School, a Dutch style of design heavily influenced by Art Nouveau, was created.

Afterwards the architecture of the internationally respected Gerrit Rietveld and Jacobus Oud inspired a new generation of contemporary architects, represented by Van Eyk, Blom and Hertzberger.

Amsterdam contains some very beautiful examples of 19th and 20th century architecture, although many regard the recent extension of the Bijlmermeer-area as the proof that now modern large-scale building has failed.

Rijksmuseum and **Centraal Station**; respectively built 1876-85 and 1881-89 by Petrus J. H. Cuypers, Dutch major exponent of neo-gothic and neo-renaissance architecture. Most of Cuypers buildings are churches. One of them is the now neglected **Vondelkerk** (or **Kerk van 't Heilig Hart,** 1870) in the Vondelkerkstraat east of the Vondelpark.

Beursgebouw, Beursplein 1-3, A'dam centrum. Tram 1, 2, 4, 5, 16, 24, 25 (Dam).
Stock exchange by Hendrik P. Berlage, constructed during 1898-1903. Town-architect Berlage was the first Dutch builder to use fixed brickwalls and iron as a span in this stock exchange. Decorative-statues and ornaments are made by Zijl and Mendes da Costa; stained glass windows are designed by Jugendstil painter Derkinderen. In 1959 cracks in the floor-surface threatened the building for some time with demolition. Restoration saved the building. A statue of Berlage-by town-sculptor Hildo Krop — is placed in front of the **Wolkenkrabber,** a building however designed by Staal (see below).

American Hotel, Leidseplein, A'dam centrum. Tram 1, 5, 7, 10; bus 26.
Generally known as "Américain", this scenic hotel/restaurant based on an art-nouveau design by American/Dutch architect C. Steinigeweg was rebuilt in 1908 by Willem Kromhout, and H. G. Jansen, contemporaries of Berlage. The restaurant was until the seventies a meeting-place for writers, artists, actors and important citizens. (see also: Restaurants)

Amsterdamse School buildings.
The municipal extension-plans south and west prepared the way to this new style of building, known as the **Amsterdamse School** (1916-23).

Interior Burgerzaal of the Palace on Dam-square

Young architects of those days shared Berlage's choice of "honest" building materials like brick, wood, stone in combination with crafts, but they rejected his sober, rationalistic way of building. The Amsterdamse School group flirted slightly with Art-nouveau principles, using many ornaments. Brick-walls were regarded and built as if they were draperies hung around concrete constructions, the main lay-out of the facade being symmetrical, while details like doors and windows are strikingly a-symmetrical. The highly decorative fronts of building-blocks are obstinate and attractive to look at; the houses themselves are small, dark and not so very comfortable to live in. Next to houses also bridges, public lavatories and stands were built in the Amsterdamse School style, mostly decorated by small, attractive, mythical sculptures made by Hildo Krop. The most typical examples of Amsterdam School houses are listed on a special map, edited by the Stedelijk Museum. Available only at the Stedelijk.

The Scheepvaarthuis (Shipping-house), Prins Hendrikkade 108, A'dam centrum. Bus 22, 32, 33, 34.
Now used as Ticket-office of the GVB, the Amsterdam Public Transport Company, the Scheepvaarthuis is regarded as the first specimen of Amsterdam School building. Its architects are De Klerk/v. d. Mey/Kramer, who built it in 1916. Decoration refers to the trade with the East and West Indies.

Building block of **"De Dageraad"**, P. L. Takstraat 1-29, A'dam zuid. Tram 12, 25 (F. Bolstraat/Churchilllaan) or tram 4 (Van Woustraat/J. Israelskade, Rijnbar).
Most striking Amsterdam School building-block built on behalf of Amsterdam socialist housing-union "Daybreak" by De Klerk and Kramer in 1920-22. They also built the area round Burgemeester Tellegenstraat, Henri Bonnerplein, Thérèse Schwartzplein and Jozef Israelskade.

Public library, Nurses Home "Lydia", Roelof Hartplein, A'dam zuid. Tram 3, 5, 12.
Other Amsterdamse School buildings in Spaarndammerbuurt, A'dam west. Bus 22 (terminal), Hembrugstraat, Hoofdweg 136-232, A'dam west. Tram 13; bus 15, are worth the trip.

Nederlandsche Handelsmaatschappij-building, Vijzelstraat 32, A'dam centrum. Tram 16, 24, 25.
Now used as head-office of the ABN bank, the building was built by K. P. C. de Bazel and A. van Gendt, post-Amsterdam School architects: there are embellishments but overall the building is simple in design.

Wolkenkrabber, Victorieplein 45, A'dam zuid. Tram 4, 12, 25. Holland's first sky-scraper (wolkenkrabber), only twelve floors high, shocked the public at first sight in 1931. The statue of town-architect Berlage in front of the building is somewhat misplaced, as the Wolkenkrabber was designed by Jan F. Staal, former Amsterdam School architect. Staal also built the American-looking former Telegraaf **Newspaper-building,** N. Z. Voorburgwal 225 (tram 1, 2, 5).

Rietveld Metz-koepel, Keizersgracht 455, A'dam centrum. Tram 1, 2, 5 (Leidsestraat).
Gerrit Rietveld (1888-1964) and Oud were the most important architects of the Netherlands, members of the internationally renowned De Stijl-group around painter Piet Mondrian. They preferred "aesthetic functionalism", using primary colours. Oud only built in Rotterdam, while Rietveld's most famous creation the **Schröder house** — can be found in Utrecht. The cupola of the Metz store is Rietveld's only design of this De Stijl period: 1933. From this cupola you can enjoy a free view on the canal-zone round Leidsestraat, but don't let the elevator-exit surprise you.

The arts and crafts-school, Gerrit Rietveld Academie, Fred Roeskestraat 96, A'dam zuid. Tram 6, 16, 24 (walk from terminal).
Also built by Rietveld dates from 1957. Nowadays one of his sons, Jan, teaches interior-architecture and design there. A private villa, in Buitenveldert reflects the main lines and colours of Rietvelds' concept, as used

Inside the Rietveld cupola, Metz building (1933), Leidsestraat

in his famous Schröder Huis. You'll find it on **Weldam 10,** A'dam Buitenveldert. Bus 23 (A. J. Ernststraat).

The Van Gogh-museum was only sketched by Rietveld and further worked out by Van Dillen and Van Tricht, as it was completed in 1972, eight years after his death.

Openluchtschool, Cliostraat 36-40, A'dam zuid. Tram 24 (Olympiaplein).
This open-air school was built in 1930 after the principles of the De 8 Opbouw groep, who pretend to be non-aesthetic, non-dramatic, non-romantic and anti-cubism as a reaction towards both Amsterdam School and De Stijl-building. This school represents the New-Objectivity way of building: clear facades with steel, glass, isolated from concrete pillars, loggia and terraces. Its creator Jan Duiker also built the revolutionary Cineac-cinema in 1934, Reguliersbreestraat near the Muntplein. This cinema is opposite the Art Nouveau cinema-palace Tuschinski, which is only 13 years older.

Het ronde blauwe theehuis, Vondelpark, A'dam zuid. Tram 6 (Amstelveenseweg).
New Objectivity round tea-house from H. Baanders, completed in 1937. (see: Tea and lunchrooms)

Moederhuis, Plantage Middenlaan 133, A'dam oost. Tram 9, 14.
The multi-colored home for single parents and their children, officially named the Hubertus Huis but known as "Mothershome", was built in 1978 by Aldo Van Eyck (born 1918), one of Hollands most renowned architects. The chosen rainbow-colours indicate the children's departments on each of the five floors.

Aldo van Eyck's "new functionalism" inspired by Rietveld also built the **Burgerweeshuis,** the **Orphans Home,** near the Amstelveenseweg and IJsbaan-pad camping. This home includes eight pavilions with inner courts as a kind of "casbah". Near the Burgerweeshuis you'll also find Rietveld's Rietveld Academie (Tram 16, 6 and 24 stop near the Olympic

Cascade-building overlooking the Zuiderkerksplein

Stadium and walk from there in southern direction across the Amstelcanal). Like most other non-public buildings the Burgerweeshuis and Moederhuis strictly don't admit visitors!

Other recently built places of architectural interest are:

Hertzberger's Montessorischool (1982), Apollolaan near Hilton Hotel (tram 16, De Lairessestraat); **Theo Bosch' Letterenfakulteit** (1984), the faculty of Literature, Singel (tram 1, 2, 5, 13 N. Z. Voorburgwal, post office).

Both architects, more or less influenced by Van Eyck also built the new parts of the **Nieuwmarkt-area** near the metro-station.

An architectural wonder to be is the **Stopera-building,** where opera and ballet will be performed. At the same time the building will serve as Townhall. The Stopera (St-adhuis/Opera-building) is located on the

Waterlooplein and will be completed in 1986. Both location and design — by Dam and Holzbauer — caused protest and even street-fights. Now the architects promise their building will be the most beautiful building in Europe, especially during evening-sessions when the lights of the Stopera are reflected in the nearby Amstel river.

PRINTSHOPS, PRINT PUBLISHERS AND ARTISTS WORKSHOPS

Listed workshops print lithographs, screenprints and etchings, sometimes also wood-cuts in cooperation with the artists. Editions, number of prints are determined by mutual arrangement. In some cases the printer also sells and exhibits work printed in his work-shop.

Steendrukkerij Amsterdam, Rento Brattinga, Lauriergracht 80, A'dam centrum (Jordaan). Telephone 241491. Tram 13 (Westermarkt).
Lithograph-printing, also irregular exhibitions.

Pieter Brattinga, Prinsengracht 628, A'dam centrum. Telephone 224265. Tram 16, 24, 25 (Vijzelstraat).
Various graphic techniques and special fast lithograph-press for poster-printing. The work-shop includes a gallery, open Mon-Fri 11-4.

Henderson, Elandsstraat 147, A'dam centrum (Jordaan). Telephone 235264. Tram 7, 10 (Marnixstraat, police office).
Screenprint and artists-workshop. Ink on paper, information phone 241491 or 167986. Publisher of graphic arts in limited editions by contemporary artists.

Workshop of lithographer Marcel Kalksma of Polychrome, Frans Halsstraat

Polychrome graphics, Frans Halsstraat 9, A'dam zuid. Telephone 794745. Tram 16, 24, 25 (Ferdinand Bolstraat/Stadhouderskade).
Recently opened print-shop with gallery. Experienced lithograph-printer Marcel Kalksma worked together with Dutch artists Cremer, Constant, Gubbels, Lataster, Lucassen, Raveel and many others. Gallery showing editions printed by him. Open Tue-Sat 1-6.

Printshop, Prinsengracht 845, A'dam centrum. Telephone 251656. Tram 16, 24, 25 (Vijzelstraat).
For more than 15 years master-printer Piet Clement and his assistants have printed lithographs, etchings, screenprints and sometimes woodcuts. Clements printshop accept print orders by Dine, Paolozzi, Hockney and Vasarely. Among Dutch artists are Cassée, Montijn, Henneman, Mutsaers and Diederen, who printed their editions here. Gallery open Mon-Sat 10-1 and 2-5.30.

Paul Schouten, Laurierstraat 60, A'dam centrum (Jordaan). Telephone 249269. Tram 13 (Westermarkt).
Schoutens Atelier "Sericus" screen-printing workshop.

Artists workshops

Het Amsterdams Grafisch Atelier, Anjeliersstraat 155A, A'dam centrum (Jordaan). Telephone 252186. Tram 13 (Westermarkt).
The Grafisch Atelier is a collective print work-shop, open to professional artists, who pay by the day. You can use the screenprint, etching and lithograph-presses and studio equipment; paper, zinc and ink have to be brought by the artists themselves. Litho-stones available. Sometimes the Grafisch Atelier takes part in collective exhibitions. Open daily from 10-6, week-ends and (school)holidays closed. Before working, contact one of the manager/artists: Mr. Rob van der Vijgh, Mr. Coos Dieters or Mrs. Ingrid Bouws.

Studio of painter

Thoets, Nassaukade 321, A'dam west. Telephone 183543. Tram 17 (Kinkerstraat).
Smaller collective graphic workshop. Sometimes studio-workshop available. Contact Mr. Jan Baas or one of his colleagues. Thoets included a small gallery with regular exhibitions by its members.

Grafische en Keramische Werkplaats Zaanstad, Veenpolderdijk 6, Assendelft-Zaanstad. Telephone 02987-4456.
Collective graphic and ceramics work-shop in Zaanstaad, 15 kms north of Amsterdam. Contact Mr. Peter Louman.

Ateliers 63, Zijlsingel 6, Haarlem. Telephone 023-321375.
Studio/workshops open to young visual artists who have spent at least three years at an academy or similar art school. Ateliers 63 set up and managed by major Dutch artists Dibbets, Beutener, van Elk, Visser is meant to be the last stage before an independent career as an artist. The conditions of entry are rather severe; applications are accepted during the whole year.

Keramisch werkcentrum Heusden, Pelschestraat 13-15, P.O. Box 15, 5256 ZG Heusden (Noord-Brabant). Telephone 04162-1694.
Ceramic work-centre, where professional (or studying) artists can develop their abilities and build up their own collection. Contact Mr. Hans van Wijck.

Montevideo, Buiksloterweg 5, A'dam noord. Telephone 237101. Ferry across the IJ behind Central Station.
Audio-visual workshop and video-gallery. Non-commercial studio, cutting-room, hire of audio-visual equipment, strictly for use by artists. f 100,- (individual/day) and f 250,- (groups/day). Just phone the mentioned telephone-number above.

USEFUL ART ADDRESSES

Artists-unions

Artists-unions have different political backgrounds, contributions, depending on specialisation and social position of the artists.
In some cases art students can apply, to be probationary members. Being a member of an artists-union can help you to get loans, subsidies and grants by the government.

Nederlandse Kring van Beeldhouwers, Mr. Stormstraat 17, 5041 CN Tilburg. Telephone 013-359163/353401.
Dutch circle of sculptors; aspiring members must be sculptors in the broadest sense of the word.

Beroepsvereniging van Beeldende Kunstenaars, BBK, Koggestraat 7, P.O. Box 10326, 1001 EH A'dam. Telephone 235456.
Union of visual artists, playing a active part in actions against government restrictions on BKR (State Aid). *BBK-krant* is their publication, special advertisements about studio-rent included.

Beroepsvereniging van Beeldende Kunstenaars BBK '69, Palmdwarsstraat 40, P.O. Box 10349, 1001 EH A'dam. Telephone 244868.
Union of visual artists, who in 1969 split up from BBK, as the result of a disagreement, concerning the occupation of the Nightwatch-hall in the Rijksmuseum.
   Aspiring members must be professional and send twelve photographs or slides of their work chosen by ballot. *BBK '69 Bulletin.*

Kunstenbond FNV, Vakgroep Beeldende Kunsten, Passeerdersgracht 32 iii 1016XR A'dam. Telephone 220025.
Union of performing and visual artists. Aspiring-members must be professional or fill a post in the arts. Publication: *Kunstenkrant* and Bulletin.

Nederlandse vakgroep Keramisten NVK, Emmerweg 3, 7722 LH Dalfsen (Overijsel). Telephone 05293-3934.
Ceramic-artists union; also students can apply. *"Keramiek"* is publication of NVK.

Vereniging van Edelsmeden en Sieraadontwerpers VES, P.O. Box 791, 1000 AT Amsterdam.
Union of makers of jewellery, goldsmiths, ornament makers, publishing VES information-bulletin.

Beroepsvereniging Fotografen, GKf, Nieuwe Keizersgracht 58, 1018 DT Amsterdam. Telephone 266571. Union of Photographers. GKf bulletin.

Beroepsvereniging, Grafische Vormgevers, GVN, Nieuwe Keizersgracht 58 sous, 1018 DT A'dam. Telephone 244748.
Union of graphic designers, publishes *Buroberichten.*

Beroepsvereniging van Nederlandse Interieur Architecten, BNA, Keizersgracht 321, P.O. Box 19610, 1000 GP A'dam. Telephone 254959.
Union of interior designers. Aspirant-members must have at least had 3 years professional experience or be registered in the "Register van Interieurarchitekten". *Interne Medelingen* is publication of BNA.

Kring Industriële Ontwerpers, K10, Lassuslaan 45, 3723 LH Bilthoven (Utrecht). Telephone 030-785281.
Circle of industrial, graphic and textile designers, also students can apply. Publication: *Bulletin and Info-berichten.*

Stichting Vrouwen in de Beeldende Kunst, SVBK, Keizersgracht 10, 1015 CN A'dam. Telephone 266589.
Women artists foundation, also taking care of organization exhibitions in Amazone gallery.

Exhibition-unions

Exhibition-unions of Amsterdam organize yearly exhibitions in the New Wing of the Stedelijk Museum, van Beerlestraat.

Nederlandse Kring van Tekenaars, Plantage Muidergracht 19, 1018 TK A'dam. Telephone 223932.
Exhibition-circle of Draughtsmen.

Nederlandse vereniging van Zeeschilders, Boulevard 27, 1931 CM Egmond aan Zee (Noord-Holland). Telephone 02206-1564. Marine-painters.

De Brug, Molenkade 40B, 1115 AC Duivendrecht. Telephone 020-940787.

Hollandse Aquarellistenkring, Van Breestraat 101 huis, 1071 ZJ A'dam. Telephone 716052.
Dutch society of water-colourists.

De Keerkring, Zomerdijkstraat 24 II, 1079 XC A'dam. Telephone 445445.

Maatschappij Arti & Amicitae, Rokin 112, 1012 LB A'dam. Telephone 233509.
Union "Art & Friendship" with own club, restaurant, café and 19th century exhibition-room, where Salons are held. Also small gallery (Arti-galerie, see: Commercial galleries).

De Onafhankelijken, Pakingehof 1, 1069 XG A'dam.

Sint Lucas, Raphaelplein 33, 1077 PX A'dam. Telephone 626407.

Stuwing, Lomanstraat 40, 1075 RC A'dam. Telephone 792226.

Time Based Arts, Bloemgracht 121, A'dam centrum (Jordaan). Telephone 229754. Tram 13, 14, 17 (Rozengracht).
Society of video-artists. TBA presents, distributes, promotes records, books, leaflets with emphasis on video. Video-artists can join TBA by producing a video or record or cassette and paying a f 100,- membership a year. TBA helps its members with several advices: finding studio's helping to produce video-tapes in Montevideo studio's. Contact Mr Aart van Barneveld.

Universal Moving Artists, Weesperzijde 75, 1091 EH A'dam. Telephone 938638.
Non-traditional and therefore one of the really surprising artists-exhibition unions.

STUDIOS

Reasonably priced studios are very hard to find in Amsterdam and neighbouring surroundings. Many young artists squat or rent old warehouses in industrial zones near the harbour or deserted factories in the city. Sometimes art-groups can offer a temporary work space for a short time, which can be useful in making projects together or in discussing each others work. Unions of visual artists publish advertisements with available studios *(BBK-krant).*

The official way to get your own studio/house is to be registered as a professional artist and a home-seeking citizen'. You receive an "urgentiebewijs", a proof you desperately need accommodation, handed out after visiting the Gemeentelijke Dieust Herhuisvesting. New buildings in Amsterdam contain at least one expensive-studio, which can be rented.

Stichting Woon-en Werkruimten voor Kunstenaars, St. Agnietenstraat 2, 1012 EG A'dam centrum. Telephone 5523386. Tram 4, 16, 24, 25 (Rokin/Muntplein).
Living/work accommodation for artists. Very friendly and willing, but unfortunately unable to help you within five years, especially if you don't want to rent an expensive newly-built house in Amsterdam-Reigersbos. Consult only on Monday morning from 9.30-11.30.

Gemeentelijke Dienst Herhuisvesting, Van Reigersbergenstraat 2, A'dam west. Telephone 806806. Bus 14, 21 (Hugo de Grootplein). Crowded, municipal housing-office.

Other useful art addresses

De Appel, Brouwersgracht 196, A'dam centrum. Telephone 255651. Tram/bus/metro: walk from Central Station, direction Haarlemmerstraat, parallel with Brouwersgracht. *57*
De Appel introduced "performance-art" to the Netherlands. Tape library of the period 1975-1980. Also literature and documentation (books, tapes, magazines). Projects of special interest are organized together with artists, on site. Specific locations, dealing with art and science, art and mass-media. Conferences and symposia are held on current topics. The foundation is open to suggestions about projects, and also willing to give advice to artists. De Appel (apple) publishes its own Dutch/English magazine, which supports the activities. (see: Art magazines). Contact Saskia Bos or Sabrina Kamstra.

Multi-Art Points, Herengracht 270, A'dam centrum. Telephone 226382. Tram 13, 17 (Westermarkt).
Open by appointment and on Saturdays from 1-6. Files of unrealised or only published plans, sketches of conceptual or concrete art. M.A.P. publishes and organises installations. Contact Mr. Bob de Wit.

Kunst en Bedrijf, J. W.B. Brouwersplein 21, 1071 LM A'dam zuid. Telephone 765198. Tram 3, 5, 12; bus 26 (van Baerlestraat, Concertgebouw). Advice and information centre about visual artists. Documentation department of Dutch artists. Kunst en Bedrijf is intermediary between monumental artists and trade, industry and municipality.

Stichting Auteursrecht, Keizersgracht 696, A'dam centrum. Telephone 223497.
STAA, First Dutch foundation, specialises in solving problems concerning international copyrights of artists, journalists, designers, TV & filmmakers. Consulting-hours: every Tuesday and Wednesday 2-4. f.25 an hour.

Stichting Beeldrecht, Nieuwe Keizersgracht 58, 1018 DT A'dam centrum. Telephone 277147.
Copyright protection for visual artists. Similar foundation for photographers: same address Burafo. Telephone 233457. 5 yr membership, 25% commission.

Stichting Materiaalfonds voor Beeldende Kunst, P.O. Box 48, 1190 AA Ouderkerk aan de Amstel. Telephone 02963-3228.
Interest-free loans for projects by artists, who are members of an artists-union.

Stichting Voorzieningsfonds voor Kunstenaars, Vvk, Noordeinde 94A, 2514 GM The Hague. Telephone 070-460826.
Insurances for artists in financial trouble. Applications only via artists-unions. Also interest-free loans for shows, materials, and to improve studios/work-shops.

Stichting Artec, Kloveniersburgwal 49, 1011 KX A'dam centrum. Telephone 241921.
Intermediary foundation between artistic, scientific and experimental projects, their creators and institutions who can help them.

STATE AID AND SUBSIDIES

The State of the Netherlands and her provincial authorities support Dutch-born artists or Dutch-based foreigners who studied in Holland. Therefore the social security for visual artists (BKR) as well as individual subsidies (e.g. Royal Subsidie), can only be of use if you are a Dutch resident.

Raad voor de kunst, Schimmelpennincklaan 3, 2517 JN The Hague. Telephone 070-469619.
Dutch Art Council, gives advice to the Minister of Welfare, Health and Culture (Welzijn, Volksgezondheid en Cultuur: WVC).

Kunstzaken Gemeente Amsterdam, Townhall, O. Z. Voorburgwal 274, A'dam centrum. Telephone 020-5529111.
Municipal Art, contact Mr. A. W. J. M. Jansen. Gives information also about various purchases by the Amsterdam Municipality.

Beeldende Kunstenaars Regeling (BKR) Amsterdam, Overschiestraat 57, 1062 HN A'dam. Telephone 5110321.
Mr. P. Bouman. Administration State Aid BKR.
Nieuwe Kerkstraat 126, A'dam centrum. Telephone 264416.
Mr. F. J. Dijk. Place, where artists hand in their BKR work.

Thanks to the BKR-support two post-war generations of visual artists were able to start their career. The State/BKR support was set up after the Second World War. Professional artists could exchange their work for social security payments, and material/studio-hire compensation. Only in Sweden and Cuba a similar art-support system seems to exist. Nevertheless the Government decided in 1984 that only artists, who have a regular income, based on sold work or a salary as an art-teacher, are allowed to apply to BKR. This decision, made to decrease the large number of dependent BKR-artists, was the result of simple measures to economize. Protests and even occupations of Rijks, Van Gogh and Stedelijk Museum and other museums in Holland by BKR artists did not prevent the accomplished fact of cutting down BKR expenses.

Nederlandse Kunststichting, P.O. Box 1258, 1000 BG A'dam. Telephone 220414.
The Dutch Art Foundation publishes a regular bulletin: BK-bulletin, where information about prizes, grants, public projects is given. Next to this the Foundation organizes travelling exhibitions of Dutch contemporary art. Only professional artists receive the BK-bulletin, after being officially registered by the Culturele Raad Noord-Holland (Cultural Council of the Province North-Holland) P.O. Box 163, 1970 AD IJ muiden. Telephone 02550-16941.

The **Staatsuitgeverij** publishes a Dutch written manual for visual artists: *Handboek Beeldende Kunst,* containing information about prizes, grants, subsidies, and important Dutch art addresses. The Handbook (Manual) is available in specialized book-shops, its international book-number is ISBN 90-12-0350-9.

PRIVATE SUBSIDIES, GRANTS AND ART PRIZES

Thérèse van Duyl-Schwartze Foundation, Meander 1041, 1181 WP Amstelveen. Telephone 020-455643.
Irregularly awarded money-prize and St. Lucas gold-metal for talented portrait-painting. In 1981 portrait-painter Herman Gordijn was awarded this prize, because of his portrait of Ivo Samkalden, former Burgomaster of Amsterdam. Afterwards Gordijn painted the portrait of Her Majesty Queen Beatrix.

Sikkens-Prijs, Rijksstraat 31, P.O. Box 3, 2170 BA Sassenheim. Telephone 01711-82627.
Prize awarded by Sikkens a Dutch colour-factory, producing industrial paint. The prize is awarded to stimulate scientific, social and cultural developments in society, in which the use of colour plays a major role.
  Among the awarded artists are Peter Struycken, major Dutch video/monumental artist and Ettore Scola, the Italian film-maker.
  Also regular Piet Mondrian readings to accompany the Sikkens-prijs activities. The purpose of this is to give more attention to the visual art, as they relate to other disciplines.

ARTISTS MATERIALS/ART TRANSPORT/INSURANCE

FINE ARTS AND GRAPHIC ARTS

Van Beek, Stadhouderskade 63-64, A'dam zuid. Telephone 621670. Tram 16, 24, 25.
Van Beek is located in a strategic place between Rijksmuseum and Rijksacademie van Beeldende Kunsten. Since the beginning of this century Van Beek has sold brushes, oil (and acrylic) paint, pigments, palettes, paper, stretchers, canvases, books, books, passe-partouts and other, graphic materials. Various branches.

Peter van Ginkel, Warmoesstraat 145, A'dam centrum. Telephone 238985. Tram 1, 2, 4, 5, 12, 14, 16, 24, 25 (Dam). Most art materials, but specialises in print-making: print-papers, inks, etching and lithographic tools, waxes, litho-stones as well as complete etching/lithographic presses. Also branch in Arnhem.

A. J. van der Linde, Rozengracht 38, A'dam centrum (Jordaan). Telephone 242791. Tram 13.
Both artists and technical drawing and other art-materials. Also hobby-materials.

Hoopman, Marnixstraat 53, A'dam centrum. Telephone 246045. Tram 7, 10.
Prepared canvases, stretchers and other art applies.

Artel, Jacobstraat 6, Haarlem. Telephone 023-327930.
Although not in Amsterdam, but in Haarlem, Artel is worth visiting for its artists-run cash & carry-like shop with a great variety of materials. The

Materials of lithographer; gum Arabic, sponge and Japanese brush

prices are generally lower than elsewhere. In Artel, housed in a former reformed church in the center of Haarlem near a large parking-garage, you can buy most art materials and equipment: The proverbial pencil-sharpener as well as a huge easel or etching-press. Also branches in major Dutch cities.

PAPER

J. Vlieger, Halvemaansteeg 4-6, A'dam centrum. Telephone 235834. Tram 4, 9, 14, 16, 24, 25 (Munt-plein).
Specialised paper shop, passe-partout card-boards and all (im)possible varieties in this specific field. Also art-materials.

BOOK BINDING

Emmerig, Van Ostadestraat 159, A'dam zuid. Telephone 710704. Tram 3, 12, 24, 25 (Ceintuurbaan/F. Bolstraat).
Book-binding materials: block-presses, knives, glues, papers, scissors, gilding, letters, litho-stones.

Saskia Roos, Leliegracht 21 sous, A'dam centrum (Jordaan). Telephone 233325. Tram 13 (Westermarkt).
Cartonnage, hand-made "marble-paper" and other book-binding papers. Printer of art books, artists books, catalogues and posters.

BOOK AND CATALOGUE PRINTER

Mart Spruyt BV, Dynamostraat 7, A'dam Havens West. Telephone 849495. Bus 28, 40 (Hemweg/Kabelweg).
This printer can help you when you like to have your own-designed poster or artist-book printed. Printer of art books, artists books, catalogues and posters.

PRINTMAKING, ZINC

Granaat, Oude Schans 11, A'dam centrum. Telephone 244525. Tram: walk from Central Station eastwards or bus 22, 32, 33, 34, 35 (Prins Hendrikkade, Montelbaans-tower).

A traditional zinc and other metals (wholesale-) trader on Oude Schans, a scenic canal-zone near Nieuwmarkt.

Wildschut, Marnixkade 109, A'dam centrum. Telephone 223158. Tram 3, 10 (Marnixstraat/Frederik Hendrikplantsoen).
Plumbers wholesale trade. Zinc-plates.

Surie & Lingeman, Rhôneweg 44, A'dam Havens West. Telephone 116755. Bus 40, 42 (Rasisweg)
Zinc-plates wholesale trade in western industrial harbour zone of the city. Only large quantities can be ordered.

Peter van Ginkel, Warmoesstraat 145, A'dam centrum. Telephone 238985. Tram 1, 2, 4, 5, 12, 14, 16, 24, 25 (Dam).
Next to graphic materials: litho-stones.

PHOTOGRAPHY/PROFESSIONAL LABS/EQUIPMENT

Alberts print service, Keizersgracht 635, A'dam centrum. Telephone 224719. Tram 16, 24, 25 (Vijzelstraat).
Colour, b/w processing, printing, inlaying, screening.

Capi-Lux Vaklaboratorium, Basisweg 42, A'dam Havens West. Telephone 111555. Bus 40, 42.
Colour, b/w processing, printing, hand-enlarging, slide-prints, retouch, delivery: 2-5 days. Professional photographic and audio-visual equipment, materials. Special editing video-room. Capi is also willing to help with all possible ideas and plans of visual artists. Founder of the Capi-firm was the father of Dutch "grey eminence" filmer Joris Ivens.

Kleurgamma, Falckstraat 49, A'dam centrum. Telephone 255562. Tram 7, 10 (Weteringschans/Frederiksplein).
Colour lab

Mammoet-foto, 2e Schinkelstraat 39-43, A'dam zuid. Telephone 718085. Tram 6, 16, 24 (Amstelveenseweg).
Printing, enlarging, reproducing, series-printing, mounting, litho montage.

S-Color, Singel 356, A'dam centrum. Telephone 221570. Tram 13 (Westermarkt/Raadhuisstraat).
Open daily fast b/w and colour developing and printing service. Open 8-10, also on Sundays.

Tripcolor, N. Z. Voorburgwal 61, A'dam centrum. Telephone 240286. Tram 1, 2, 5, 13, 17.
Processing of E6, Kodak, Agfachrome CK1, slide-duplicates, colour, b/w enlarging.

VB fototechniek, Weesperstraat 101, A'dam centrum. Telephone 233291. Tram 3, 6, 7, 10 (Sarphatistraat, Weesperplein), metro Weesperplein.
Processing, reproducing, line-print.

Miscellaneous:

One Hour Photo Service, F. Bolstraat 99, A'dam zuid. Telephone 715583. Tram 16, 24, 25.
Other branches in Leidsestraat 81A, A'dam centrum. Telephone 253673. Tram 1, 2, 5 and Rokin 106, A'dam centrum. Telephone 256294. Tram 1, 2, 4, 16, 24, 25.
Only colour processing and printing within two hours.

Camex, Parnassusweg 204, A'dam zuid. Telephone 620188. Bus 26.
Cash and carry photographic equipment, free colour film when colour-processing and printing, second hand and old-time camera's. Also branch in Zaandam.

De Econoom, Nieuwendijk 97, A'dam centrum. Telephone 233904. Tram 4, 9, 16, 24, 25 (Damrak).
Purchase of used camera's, also tax-free equipment.

Professional, Nieuwendijk 113, A'dam centrum. Telephone 246024. Tram 4, 9, 16, 24, 25 (Damrak).
Leica-Hasselblad dealer, purchase of photo-equipment.

Camera-repair

Kiekie, Ouddiemerlaan 16, Diemen. Telephone 020-995169. Metro. Diemen.
Camera-repair.

Nagami, Oude Leliestraat 16, A'dam centrum. Telephone 260643. Tram 13 (Raadhuisstraat).
Specializes in repair of Nikon camera's, also Japanese curiosity shop.

Rector, Zeilstraat 54, A'dam west. Telephone 730019. Tram 2, 6, 16 (Amstelveenseweg); bus 15.
First and second-hand camera repair.

COPIERS

Canon, Gebouw 70, Schiphol-Oost. Telephone 020-472634. Bus CN 196, 142, 173, 174 (departing from several Amsterdam railway stations).
Schiphol Oost (east) is the former airport, now used for industrial transport.
Canon introduced colour-copy as an art in Holland. You can hire the colour-copy machine by the hour or pay for every copy you make. When hiring please phone for appointment. Some years ago Canon published an edition with contemporary colour-copy art, made by Giele, Lindhout, Veldhoen, Panhuyzen and others.

Grand Prix Copy, Parnassusweg 218, A'dam zuid. Telephone 645909. Bus 26.

Grand Prix Copy, Weteringschans 84A, A'dam centrum. Telephone 272703. Tram 7, 10.
Do it yourself copy-service, low prices, also colour-copy.

Printerette Jubels bv, Van Eeghenlaan 1, A'dam zuid. Telephone 627066. Tram 2, 3, 5, 12 (Constantijn Huygensstraat, Stedelijk Museum).

Printerette, Vijzelstraat 70, A'dam centrum. Telephone 254604. Tram 16, 24, 25.

Printerette, Spuistraat 91, A'dam centrum. Telephone 272425. Tram 13 (Raadhuisstraat).
Another do it yourself service. Also chroma-colour-copy service, off-set, text-composing.

AUDIO-VISUAL

RUAD, Overtoom 371, A'dam west. Telephone 126848. Tram 1, 2, 6.
Hiring or selling film, audio-visual equipment.

Stampij, Warmoesstraat 145, A'dam centrum. Telephone 277426. Tram 1, 2, 4, 5, 12, 24, 25 (Dam).
Hiring, montage, U-matic recording sets.

Open Studio, Zoutkeetsgracht 114, A'dam west. Telephone 243720. Tram 3 (terminal).
Hiring of video-tapes and equipments.

Montevideo, Buiksloterweg 5, A'dam noord. Telephone 237101. Tram/bus: take ferry right behind the Central Station and cross the IJ-harbour, Montevideo is the first building at your left. Non-commercial hiring of all audio-visual equipment, studio specialised in video-art.
Costs: f 100,- (individual/day) and f 250,- (groups/day) studio/equipment hire. (see also: Artists workshops and Artists spaces).

SCULPTURE

Metals/Steel/Iron/Aluminium

Granaat, Oude Schans 11, A'dam centrum. Telephone 244525. Bus 22, 32, 33, 34, 35 (Prins Hendrikkade, Montelbaanstower).

Surie & Lingeman, Rhôneweg 44, A'dam Havens West. Telephone 116755. Bus 40, 42 (Basisweg) Western industrial harbour-zone.
Further, try scrap-iron traders, some are willing to let you trace their supply. Addresses are mentioned in the Gouden Gids/Yellow Papers telephone guide: Oude metalen (Old metals).

Tools
Gunters & Meuser, Egelantiersgracht 2-6, A'dam centrum (Jordaan). Telephone 221666. Tram 13 (Westermarkt).

Stone
Cortlever Agricola BV, Van der Madeweg 18, A'dam Overamstel. Telephone 650567/921712. Bus 41.
You can also try the tombstone companies at graveyards.

Clay
Veka, Bloemgracht 132, A'dam centrum (Jordaan). Telephone 248526. Tram 7, 10 (Marnixstraat/Elandsgracht).

Silex, de Meerheuvel 5, Den Bosch (Noord-Brabant). Telephone 073-215573.
All materials clay, enamels, etc. Low prices

Timber
Amsterdamse Fijnhouthandel, Bloemgracht 67, A'dam centrum (Jordaan). Telephone 245329. Tram 7, 10 (Marnixstraat/Elandsgracht, police-office).

Timber-yard of the AFH, Minervahavenweg 14, A'dam Havens West. Telephone 828079. Bus 28 (a very long walk from Tasmanstraat). Only hard-wood. Other wood-varieties available at various timber-woodshops in the city.

Polyester/Plastics/Artificial cast resins
Polyservice, Archimedesweg 64, A'dam east. Telephone 654569. Bus 8.

ABC, Sarphatistraat 136, A'dam east. Telephone 223699. Tram 3, 6, 7, 10; metro (Weesperplein).
Fabrication and selling of perspex, plexiglas, texan.

Van Buseck & Co, Derde Wittenburgerdwarsstraat 76, A'dam east. Telephone 236245/224678. Tram 6 (Wittenburgerstraat).
Perspex.

Multi-gips, Zeeburgerdijk 55 I, A'dam Havens Oost. Telephone 944040. Tram 10.
Plaster.

Bronze foundries
Fred Steffens, Kerkweg 1, Spaarnwoude (near Haarlem). Telephone 023-376666.

Volkers, Deilsedijk, Deil (Gelderland). Telephone 03457-452.

Sculptor-materials
Van Beek, Stadhouderskade 63, A'dam centrum. Telephone 621670. Tram 16, 24, 25 (Ferdinand Bolstraat).

FRAMING/DISPLAYS/SHOW-CASES

Alulijst, Kadijksplein 7, A'dam centrum. Telephone 224167. Bus 22 (scheepvaartmuseum).
Aluminium frames.

Bergsma, Anjeliersstraat 59, A'dam centrum (Jordaan). Telephone 278361. Tram 13, 14, 17 (Rozengracht).
Displays, mounts, frames, show-cases of plastic, polyester and perspex.

Jollijst, Haarlemmerstraat 110, A'dam centrum. Telephone 237300. Tram/bus/metro: walk westwards from the Central Station.
Aluminium frames, discount on large amounts and standard sizes, do-it-yourself kits.

Partout, N. Z. Voorburgwal 49, A'dam centrum. Telephone 240620. Tram 1, 2, 5, 13, 17.
Frame-factory, mouldings in different colours.

Heydenrijk, Rokin 105, A'dam centrum. Telephone 244847. Tram 4, 9, 16, 24, 25.
Specialises in framing of drawings, water-colours, graphics. Various mouldings: classic and modern.

RESTORING OF PRINTS, PAINTINGS ETC.

Van Dantzig, Chopinstraat 17, A'dam zuid. Telephone 640496. Tram 24; bus 15, 26 (Stadionweg, Beethovenstraat).

J. van Gool, Kikkenstein 162, A'dam Bijlmermeer. Telephone 995272. Bus 55, 56; metro Bijlmermeer.

J. J. Houillier, Willemsparkweg 51, A'dam zuid. Telephone 719497. Tram 2.

J. J. van Litsenburg, Pieter de Hoochstraat 20, A'dam zuid. Telephone 763988. Tram 16 (Johannes Vermeerstraat).

Schoonekamp, Lindengracht 35 huis, A'dam centrum (Jordaan). Telephone 278030. Tram 13, 14, 17 (Rozengracht).

Vroom, Herengracht 66, A'dam centrum. Telephone 224402. Tram 13 (Westermarkt).

Wil Werkoven, P. C. Hooftstraat 60, A'dam zuid. Telephone 648099. Tram 3, 12; bus 26, 67, 69.

GRAPHIC AND ARCHITECTURAL DESIGN MATERIALS

De Vijf, Lijnbaansgracht 162, A'dam centrum. Telephone 240593. Tram 7, 10 (Marnixstraat, police-office).
Drawing-office materials.

Van Beek, Weteringschans 201, A'dam centrum. Telephone 239647. Tram 7, 10.
Department of Van Beek with graphic art supplies for designers.

Vlietstra, Sarphatistraat 23, A'dam centrum. Telephone 274089. Tram 3, 6, 7, 10; metro (Weesperplein).

CERAMICS

Veka, Bloemgracht 132, A'dam centrum (Jordaan). Telephone 248526. Tram 7, 10 (Marnixstraat/Elandsgracht).

Silex, de Meerheuvel 5, Den Bosch (Noord-Brabant). Telephone 073-215573.
Clay, enamels, furnaces etc. Also equipment.

Keramisch instituut, Wapenweg 12, Haarlem. Telephone 023-327525.
Pottery-wheels, furnaces, clay, enamels.

FABRICS

Naturel, Gasthuismolensteeg 4, A'dam centrum. Telephone 223751. Tram 1, 2, 4, 9, 16, 24, 25 (Dam square).
Natural-coloured fabrics, pure wool, linen, cotton, silk, dye-powder, yarns solid by weight. Also spinning-wheels. Textile-artists buy their materials here.

Wool shop 'Naturel' in Gasthuismolensteeg

ART TRANSPORT

Gerlach, P.O. Box 7554, Schiphol centrum. Telephone 171971.
International forwarding agents, service at home and abroad, packaging, insurance, shipping, custom formalities.

XYZ, firma L. van der Linden, Keizersgracht 826, A'dam centrum. Telephone 250145.
Transport all over Holland. XYZ is experienced in bringing work to purchase-centres in Amsterdam.

Van Gend en Loos, Cruqiuskade 25, A'dam east. Telephone 223481/235918.
Carrier-service.

TRANSPORT VAN RENT

Rent your own transport van. Some addresses are:

Diks, Van Ostadestraat 278-280, A'dam zuid. Telephone 623366. Tram 16, 24, 25 (F. Bolstraat/Ceintuurbaan).

Drive yourself, Wibautstraat 40, A'dam centrum. Telephone 947097. Metro.

Kuperus, Middenweg 175, A'dam east. Telephone 938790. Tram 9.

KAV, Johan Huizingalaan 91, A'dam Osdorp. Telephone 141435. Bus 23.

Ouke Baas, Van Ostadestraat 366, A'dam zuid. Telephone 794842. Tram 16, 24, 25 (F. Bolstraat/Ceintuurbaan).

INSURANCE

Companies that specialise in insuring art transport and/or exhibitions against loss or theft.

Blom & Van der Aa, Johannes Worpstraat 2, 1076 BG A'dam zuid. Telephone 767111. Bus 26 (Parnassusweg).

Heerkens, Thijssen & Co., Keizersgracht 224, 1016 DZ A'dam centrum. Telephone 229261. Tram 1, 2, 5, 13 (N. Z. Voorburgwal, post-office).

Smit, Boelen & Co., Nes 116-118, 1012 KE A'dam centrum. Telephone 239225. Tram 1, 2, 5, 16, 24, 25 (Rokin, Lange Brugsteeg).

ART MAGAZINES

Most art magazines cover important exhibitions of contemporary arts in Amsterdam, elsewhere in Holland and sometimes also in Germany, Belgium and France.
   Nearly all contain an art diary, but unfortunately miss an English summary.
   Average price is about f 10,-.

AKT, Oude Boteringsestraat 81, 9712 GG Groningen.
Quarterly magazine of students art history. Both current and historical art forms.

Alert, Kloveniersburgwal 115, 1011 KC Amsterdam. Monthly gallery guide. Dutch text. F3.50

De Appel, Brouwersgracht 196, 1013 HD A'dam.
Centre of performances, process-like art projects and other recent developments of modern art. Next to information about their own activities, art theoretical articles in Dutch and English, b/w illustrations. (see also: Other useful art addresses)

Arte Factum, Amerikalei 125, 3200 Antwerpen-Belgium.
Excellent, international, glossy magazine for polyglot art lovers, to read during long travels through Europe visiting all current expositions. Contains international reviews, book news. Appears 6 times a year.

Bijvoorbeeld, P.O. Box 41042, 1019 EA A'dam.
Quarterly Dutch languaged volume with general information about arts and crafts. Colour and b/w illustrations. Send diary information three months in advance to Mr. Gert Staal, Keizersgracht 135, 1015 CK Amsterdam.

Code, distributed by Art Book, Prinsengracht 645, 1016 HV Amsterdam.
Magazine, made by young Dutch and foreign artists next to their artistic activities. Irregularly published. In the heart of each volume an original screen-print or colour-copy has been folded. Dutch and English texts.

Dutch Art & Architecture Today, P.O. Box 2242, 1000 CE A'dam.
The official English bulletin, which accompanies the export of Dutch art. Informs also about (establishing) art forms in Holland, Twice a year.

Maandblad Fodor, Keizersgracht 609, 1017 DS A'dam.
Magazine, which mostly serves as additional information source about the exhibitions in Museum Fodor. Original screen-print by exhibiting artists, in each volume. Fodor appears 6 times a year.

Items, Herengracht 23, 1382 AG Weesp.
Current Dutch architectural, industrial and graphic design magazine.

Kunst & Antiek Revue, P.O. Box 85994, 2508 CR The Hague.
Glossy traditional art and antique review appearing eleven times a year.

Kunstbeeld, P.O. Box 4, 2400 MA Alphen aan de Rijn.
Largest Dutch monthly art magazine with reviews, interviews, and an enormous diary. Colour-illustrations. Send diary-information — three months in advance — to Mrs. R. Huysmans-v.d. Water, Bilderdijkstraat 39, 4819 GA Breda.

Jong Holland, P.O. Box 63, 5590 AB Heeze.
New quarterly volume, dealing with Dutch arts and crafts from 1880 until today, with an English summary.

De Kunstliefhebber, c/o Mr. Pieter Hermanides, Plantage Middenlaan 74 II, 1018 DJ A'dam.
Friendly home-made magazine by artists. Highly internationally orientated as no diary or texts are published but only pictures and drawings.

Kunstschrift, P.O. Box 5294, 1380 AG Weesp.
6 times a year. Colour volume, edited by Openbaar Kunstbezit, the foundation which takes care of artistic education. Includes diary.

Metropolis M, P.O. Box 5294, 1380 AG Weesp.
Young runner-up art magazine with special interest in the Dutch or foreign 'alternative' galleries. Appears 6 times a year. Each volume contains two pages, made by young artists.

Museumjournaal, P.O. Box 2286, 1000 CG A'dam.
Official volume of the Dutch art-museum, therefore filled with background theories about exhibiting artists. Sometimes interesting thematic issues are produced. Museumjournaal serves also as discussion-platform about 'burning' matters of art. Chief-editor is Mr. Paul Groot, who also organises expositions.

MW, P.O. Box 113, 2200 AC Noordwijk.
Recently started quarterly on modern art.

Professionele fotografie, Antwoordnummer 700, 6500 WC Nijmegen.
6 times a year. Professional photography coverage.

Outline, Oude Delft 145, 2611 HA Delft.
Quarterly publication about applied arts and handicrafts, edited by COSA foundation.

Tableau, P.O. Box 8444, 3503 RK Utrecht.
6 times a year, colourful magazine about traditional arts and antiques. Also free available aboard the Dutch KLM airplanes. Only interesting for people who visit art-auctions and for antique-dealers in Holland. Chief-editor is Mr. Jan Juffermans.

Tentoonstellingsagenda, P.O. Box 20014, 2500 EA The Hague, Official Dutch art-diary. Completely without any illustrations.

Uitkrant, Kleine Gartmanplantsoen 10, 1017 RR A'dam.
Free monthly cultural information newspaper. Contains large museum and gallery-page. Indispensable for cultural Amsterdam information.

Wonen TA/BK, Leidsestraat 5, 1017 NS A'dam.
Twice a month, a volume on architecture, town-planning and design.

Zien Magazine, P.O. Box 77, 5126 ZR Gilse.
Edited by the Stichting Pretentieus (Foundation Pretentious). Characterising the over-sized quarterly full-colour issues of Zien. Zien (see) is created by Dutch artists and art-historians, following hyper-actual streams in modern-staged photo-event-photography.
In contrary to previous issues, Dutch readers have to read their own summary of the English contents of their magazine.

De Zaak, Turftorenstraat 18-20, 9712 BP Groningen.
Quarterly, edited by a Groningen-based group of artists.

NEWSPAPER SECTIONS ON ART/ART-CRITICS

Every **Wednesday evening** newspapers turn their attention fully to art and cultural life in the city, beginning with the new cinema-programmes, published in the evening-papers of that day or in the papers appearing the next morning.

Trying to get an exhibition reviewed or even mentioned can be a very hard job indeed. Only the **Uitkrant,** with its special gallery and alternative-art-spaces diary, makes a serious attempt of listing all Amsterdam exhibitions.

Every editorial art-office gets snowed under with invitations, press-informations about current art-shows. Unfortunately for artists making their debut in unknown galleries, the quality of previous shows counts. So most of the decisions about which exhibitions to visit are made behind the — overloaded — desk in the editorial office.

Listed below are the visual arts chief editors of the Dutch newspapers and weekly magazines. Don't forget too the specialized art-press, mentioned in the previous section, although they generally are not able to cover really current events.

Newspapers

Algemeen Dagblad, Westblaak 180, P.O. Box 241, 3000 DB Rotterdam. Telephone 010-147211. Morning-paper.
Chief-editor arts-section is **Mr. Menno Schenke.** No special gallery section.

NRC Handelsblad, Westblaak 180, P.O. Box 241, 3000 DB Rotterdam. Telephone 010-147211. Evening-paper.
Editorial-office arts. N. Z. Voorburgwal 303, A'dam centrum. Telephone

254153. Regular gallery-section (weekly on Fridays), exhibition reviews, interviews. Special cultural supplement (CS) every Friday, art-diary.
Chief-editor arts: **Mrs. Lien Heyting.** Other art-journalists are **Janneke Wesseling, Betty van Garrel, Bas Roodnat, K. Schippers and Riki Simons** (freelance).

Het Parool, Wibautstraat 131, P.O. Box 433, 1000 AK A'dam. Telephone 5629333. Evening-paper.
Chief-editor arts: **Mr. Jan-Bart Klaster.** Other art-journalists are **Cathérine van Houts,** and freelance: **Frans Duister, Hennie v.d. Louw** and **Chris Reinewald.**
  No special gallery-section, but regularly reviews and interviews in cultural enclosure/diary: Amsterdam Uit en Thuis-bijlage, every Wednesday evening.

De Telegraaf, Basisweg 30, P.O. Box 376, 1000 EB A'dam. Telephone 5859111. Largest Dutch newspaper.
Mr. Ed Wingen reviews gallery and museum exhibitions every Friday morning.

Trouw, Wibautstraat 131, P.O. Box 859, 1000 AW A'dam. Telephone 5629444. Morning-paper.
Regular gallery and museum exhibition reviews by **Mr. Kees Straus.**

De Volkskrant, Wibautstraat 148, P.O. Box, 1000 BA A'dam. Telephone 5629222. Morning-paper.
Chief-editor arts: **Mr. Eric Beenker.** Gallery and exhibition reviews by freelance journalist: **Mrs. Anna Tilroe.**

De Waarheid, Hoogte Kadijk 145, P.O. Box 343, 1016 EZ A'dam. Telephone 262565. Evening-paper.
Mr. Jelle Jeensma and **Mr. Joost Dievendahl** both take care of reviewing exhibition and art-events.

Financiëel Dagblad, Weesperstraat 85, 1018 VN A'dam. Telephone 223333. Financial newspaper.
Weekly gallery-review written by **Mr. W. M. Lockman.**

Opinion-weeklies

Opinion-weeklies generally are on sale every Wednesday and following days in the news-stands.

Elseviers Magazine, Spuistraat 110, P.O. Box 152, 1000 AD A'dam. Telephone 244950.
Special section on art and culture. Chief-editor is Mr. Jan Juffermans.

De Groene Amsterdammer, Westeinde 16, P.O. Box 353, 1000 AJ A'dam. Telephone 230864.
Weekly art and culture reviews by Mr. Frank Gribling, Mr. Walter Barten and Mr. Loek Zonneveld.

Haagse Post, Singel 264, P.O. Box 1050, 1000 BB A'dam. Telephone 243576.
Regular film/literature enclosure; exhibition-reviews and interviews by Mr. Ron Kaal.

Hervormd Nederland, Scheveningseweg 72, P.O. Box 84176, 2508 AD The Hague. Telephone 070-512111.
Chief-editor arts: Mr. E. van Amerongen.

De Tijd, Stadhouderskade 85, P.O. Box 348, 1000 AH A'dam. Telephone 731361.
Chief-editor arts/culture is Mr. Ben Kroon, Mr. Philip Peeters writes about contemporary arts.

Intermagazine, Rijnsburgstraat 11, P.O. Box 9194, 1000 CC A'dam. Telephone 5102911.
Chief-editor arts: Mr. William Rothuizen.

Vrij Nederland, Raamgracht 4, P.O. Box 1050, 1000 BB A'dam. Telephone 262375.
No specific gallery or exhibition review but background stories about art and artists. Coordination contemporary arts: Miss Ella Reitsma. Diary-information about non-commercial art-events can be sent to: Affiche, P.O. Box 1391, 1000 BJ A'dam.

Other magazines, with special interest in arts:

Avenue, Stadhouderskade 85, P.O. Box 495, 1073 AT A'dam. Telephone 231375.
Monthly trend-setting magazine on fashion, (interior-) design, culinary art, cultural events. Avenue includes a monthly 'galerie Avenue' section, introducing generally visual arts and artists to her readers, and offering one work of them. Miss Anneke van Steyn is coordinator of the section.

Elegance, Naarderstraat 35, 1211 AJ Hilversum. Telephone 035-19841. P.O. Box 1807, 1200 BV Hilversum.
Monthly fashion, design cultural magazine with regular interest in the arts. Chief-editor is Mr. H. J. Bouman.

Vinyl, P.O. Box 1050. 1000 BB A'dam, Prinseneiland 52/4. Telephone 249226/227119.
Avant-garde pop music magazine with occasional reviews on rather fashionable art-exhibitions.

Amsterdam Today, Leidsekade 107, P.O. Box 12392, 1100 AJ A'dam. Telephone 222231.
English written Amsterdam magazine. Arts editor is Mr. Hennie van der Louw.

The paper, Lauriersgracht 116, A'dam centrum. Telephone 260216.
Monthly information/cultural magazine for English speaking citizens. Arts editor: Mr. Adriaan van Oosten.

Uitkrant, gallery section, send information to Mrs. Lily van Ginneken, Egelantiersgracht 55, 1015 RD A'dam. Telephone 265950.

RADIO/TV

Most broadcasting companies in Holland have a regular radio — and sometimes — television-program on contemporary arts. In some cases a diary is part of the program.

NOS, P.O. Box 1200 JB, Hilversum.
Cultural television-programs: Nederland C, and Omnibus. Chief-editors: Mr. H. Keller, Mr. Theo Stokkink and Mr. J. Walvis.

AVRO, P.O. Box 2, 1200 JA Hilversum.
Radioprogram: Kijk op kunst.

Vpro, P.O. Box 11, 1200 JC Hilversum.
Broadcasting company with special interest in avant-garde culture and arts. Chief-editor: Mr Rob Klaasman sometimes organises private-exhibitions in his Amsterdam home, Keizersgracht 431.

Radio Stad, Johannes Vermeerstraat 29, 1071 DL A'dam. Telephone 719071.
Amsterdam local radio, incidental interest in visual arts, daily cultural information.

KRO, Emmastraat 52, 1213 AL Hilversum. Catholic broadcasting company. Radioprogram: Spektakel.

TROS, P.O. Box 450, 1200 AL Hilversum.
Regular cultural radio-programs with diary.

VARA, P.O. Box 175, 1200 AD Hilversum.
Socialists broadcasting company.
Radioprogram: Het Zout In De Pap. Mrs. Jeanne van Munster is editor.

Veronica, P.O. Box 11, 1200 JC Hilversum.
Radioprogram: CRM.

ART BOOKSHOPS

All art bookshops sell books in English and German. Other languages — including Dutch — are seldom found. Like other general bookshops, art bookshops open Monday afternoon, and close only on Sunday. Rijks, Stedelijk and Van Gogh Museum each have an interesting but modest art book-department.

Art Book, Prinsengracht 645, A'dam centrum. Telephone 259337. Tram 1, 2, 5 (Leidsestraat).
Next to her own bookshop Mrs. Sakia Osterholt publishes and distributes art books. The large collection of Art Book covers modern art, photography, architecture, design, various international art-magazines and catalogues. The interior of the shop was recently designed by two young architects Sas and De Vries, who also were responsible for the extraordinary cafés Walem and Oblomov.

Erasmus, Spui 2, A'dam centrum. Telephone 230535. Tram 1, 2, 4, 5, 16, 24, 25 (Rokin).
Art books with specialisation from 17th-20th century painting, orientalia and other arts and crafts. Also books on classic and modern architecture. Erasmus includes a famous antiquarian bookshop with German literature on the first floor. You have to ring the bell before entering the shop.

Art books at Art book shop, Prinsengracht

Lankamp & Brinkman, Spiegelgracht 19, A'dam centrum. Telephone 234656. Tram 6, 7, 10 (Weteringschans, Rijksmuseum). Closes at lunchtime.
Very well assorted collection of international instruction and information books on traditional crafts from Europe, Africa and Asia etc. Next to all that a substantial bookshop with similar service. Regular window-displays on illustrated childrens-books.

Premsela, Van Baerlestraat 78, A'dam zuid. Telephone 624266. Tram 3, 5, 12; bus 26.
Art-bookshop, designed by well known Dutch interior-architect Benno Premsela, brother of Robert, founder of the company. You can't miss

Art bookshop Premsela, opposite the Stedelijk Museum, Van Baerlestraat

Premsela, as it is located opposite the New Wing of the Stedelijk Museum. Large variety of both classical and contemporary arts, crafts, fashion, ballet, photography, design. Regular, fresh import of catalogues, magazines and valuable books.

De Verbeelding, Utrechtsestraat 40, A'dam centrum. Telephone 265385. Tram 4.
Mr. Fred Schmidts collection of modern art, books, self-imported catalogues, photography, architecture. Also small exhibitions.

Architectura & Natura, Leliegracht 44, A'dam centrum. Telephone 236186. Tram (Westermarkt).
Friendly but rather chaotic bookshop, strangely enough specializing in interior-design, architecture, garden-architecture, planology and nature. Worth visiting this unique bookshop.

C. P. J. van der Peet, Nieuwe Spiegelstraat 33-35, A'dam centrum. Telephone 235763. Tram 6, 7, 10 (Weteringschans, Rijksmuseum).
Old, antique and rare books and prints on oriental arts. Interesting exhibitions of Utomaro, Hiroshige 'ukiyo-e' Japanese colour-wood-cuts.

Sud Antiquariaat, Spiegelgracht 8, A'dam centrum. Telephone 278124. Tram 6, 7, 10 (Weteringschans, Rijksmuseum).
Second-hand art books, catalogues, magazines but also new books. Mr. J. van den Brink, owner of Sud, is willing to exchange books or works of art with you. Specialisation of Sud: Cobra, Sandberg (former typographer/curator of the Stedelijk Museum) catalogues, Constructivism, De Stijl. Collection graphics and paintings by Alechinsky and other artists from the sixties.

WELL ASSORTED ART-SECTION BOOKSHOPS

Allert/De Lange, Damrak 62, A'dam centrum. Telephone 246744. Tram 4, 9, 16, 24, 25. Art book cellar.
Also large collection travel-guides and English/French/German literature department.

Athenaeum Boekhandel, Spui 14-16, A'dam centrum. Telephone 226248.
Its neighbouring newstands Athaeneum Nieuwscentrum — also opened on Sundays — sells an enormous collection of international avant-garde art and cultural magazines and leaflets.

De Moderne Boekhandel/Bas, Leidsestraat 70 I, A'dam centrum. Telephone 248169.
Also interesting 'ramsj': publishers remainders department.

Scheltema, Holkema en Vermeulen, Koningsplein 16-18, A'dam centrum. Telephone 267212. Tram 1, 2, 5.
Large collection art/design and scientific books.

Other interesting bookshops:

Van Gennep, N. Z. Voorburgwal 330, A'dam centrum. Telephone 264448. Tram 1, 2, 5.
Publishing company and bookshop. Here, on the N. Z. Voorburgwal international 'ramsj' books are sold. The collection includes some very interesting and cheap art, photography books. Regular remainders from American and British hard-back best-sellers.

De Slegte, Kalverstraat 48-52, A'dam centrum. Telephone 225933. Tram 1, 2, 5, 16, 24, 25 (Dam).
Large second-hand and remainder bookshop. Art department with cheap but generally not so well reproduced art books. The antiquarian department upstairs is more interesting to visit. De Slegte also buys the books you are fed up with.

Arcanum, Reguliersgracht 54, A'dam centrum. Telephone 250813. Tram 6, 7, 10 (Weteringschans/Frederiksplein).
Esoteric, black and white magic, oriental arts.

American Discount, Kalverstraat 158, A'dam centrum. Telephone 255537. Tram 1, 2, 4, 5, 16, 24, 25 (Dam).
Strictly English and American books and magazines, all discount-priced.

Ming Ya, Gelderskade 105, A'dam centrum. Telephone 258330. Metro (Nieuwmarkt).
Chinese contemporary crafts and arts, English translations of Chinese literature. Scenic Chinese pastel-coloured weeklies.

Island International Bookstore, 2e Tuindwarsstraat 14, A'dam centrum (Jordaan). Telephone 268509. Tram 13 (Westermarkt).
Friendly bookshop, representing alternative American literature. Regular artists' books are sold.

The English Bookshop, Laurierstraat 71, A'dam centrum (Jordaan). Telephone 264230. Tram 7, 10 (Marnixstraat, police-office).
Presentation of all major British titles, edited by Penguin and some other publishers.

José Marti, Herengracht 259 sous, A'dam centrum. Telephone 269590. Tram 13 (Westermarkt).
Latin-American, Iberian, Spanish, Portuguese-literature and records.

Libreria Bonardi, Van Oldenbarneveldtstraat 51 huis, A'dam west. Telephone 826390. Tram 7, 17 (Kinkerstraat).
Very well assorted Italian bookshop, makes you wish to be Italian.

Theatre Bookshop, Leidseplein 26A, A'dam centrum. Telephone 226489. Tram 1, 2, 5.
Books on dance, theatre, cabaret, drama, and film housed in Stadsschouwburg. Also records and cheap textbooks available.

Van Wijngaarden, Overtoom 136, A'dam west. Telephone 121901. Tram 1, 6.
Very well-specialized, geographical bookshop with over 8000 different maps, 2000 travel guides covering the whole world. Shop to visit before making your world-tour.

Music-bookshop Groen, Ferdinand Bolstraat 6, A'dam zuid. Telephone 762240. Tram 16, 24, 25.
Sheet-music, music-literature, classical music records.

Xantippe, Prinsengracht 290, A'dam centrum. Telephone 235854. Tram 13 (Westermarkt).
International women's bookshop. Literature written by women only. Exhibitions by female-artists. But no fear, men are also allowed to enter and buy.

ART POSTERS

Art Unlimited, Keizersgracht 510, A'dam centrum. Telephone 236541. Tram 1, 2, 5 (Leidsestraat).
Art posters, postcards of international artists from various centuries.

Ciné Qua Non, Staalstraat 14, A'dam centrum. Telephone 255588. Tram 4, 9, 14, 16, 24, 25 (Muntplein).
Film bookshop, Posters, stills, film theory books, scripts. Specialization: French and Italian cinema. And of course in the museums: posters, reproductions and postcards are sold.

ART LIBRARIES

Bibliotheek van het Stedelijk Museum, Paulus Potterstraat 13, A'dam zuid. Telephone 732166. Tram 2, 3, 5, 12; bus 26 (van Baerlestraat).
Open: due to construction works inside the museum, the library is opened irregularly. Phone for information to prevent disappointment. Library contains books on modern arts, crafts, graphics and international art magazines. No lending, card-index, photo-copiers.

Bibliotheek van het Rijksmuseum, Stadhouderskade 42, A'dam zuid. Telephone 732121. Tram 6, 7, 10 (Weteringschans).
Open to public daily except weekends from 10-5. No lending of books on classic arts and crafts. Highly scenic library.

Bibliotheek van het Filmmuseum, Vondelpark 3, A'dam centrum/zuid. Telephone 831646. Tram 2, 3, 5, 12 (Const. Huygensstraat, front entrance to the park.
Open Tuesday, Wednesday, Thursday from 9-5. Literature on film, scenarios, etc.

GENERAL PUBLIC LIBRARIES

General public libraries are spread over the city. You must be a member to borrow books, records or sheet-music.
All libraries (Openbare Leeszalen en Bibliotheken) **close on Thursday and Sunday.** They are also opened every evening except the before mentioned days and Saturday. Opening hours 9-6 and 7-9. The largest collection of books and records can be found at the **Openbare Bibliotheek,** Prinsengracht 587, A'dam centrum. Tram 1, 2, 5 (Leidsestraat). Telephone 265065. They also lend sheet music.

ART SCHOOLS

Gerrit Rietveld Academie, Fred. Roeskestraat 96, A'dam nieuw zuid. Telephone 620406. Tram 6, 16, 24 (walk from terminal across the Amstel-canal next to Olympic Stadium).
Post-graduate courses of 5 years, covering interior-design, industrial design, fashion, stage design, audio-visuals, photography, textiles, illustration, graphical design, graphic arts, painting, sculpture, jewellery, pottery, ceramics. Diplom Academie van Beeldende Kunsten. Day and evening-courses (largest in Holland). The syllabus of the Rietveld

Academie is more or less based on the Bauhaus theories. Conditions of entry are rather severe, because of the extremely large amount of aspiring-students. Therefore special consulting-hours are necessary before being allowed to take part in the entrance exams. Day-course consulting-hours until March, entrance examinations around April. Evening-course consulting-hours until August, entrance examinations around September. During these examinations you are requested to show your work, and invited to talk about your motivations. Students of the evening-course are generally expected to work during day-time in a similar profession. Final exams result in interesting exhibitions during the first weeks of June; the best way to know the qualities and possibilities of the Academie. Day and evening-students present (and sell) their work.

Open air casting studio of Rietveld Academie, Fred Roeskestraat

Skeleton and living artist in drawing-room of Rijksacademie, Stadhouderskade

Rijksacademie voor Beeldende Kunsten, Stadhouderskade 86, A'dam zuid. Telephone 797811. Tram 16, 24, 25 (F. Bolstraat).
The oldest and therefore classical orientated State Academy, was founded in 1870 by King Willem I. Post-graduate courses of 5 years with departments of painting, monumental arts, sculpture, graphics, visual communication, scenography. Diploma Academie van Beeldende Kunsten. Entrance examinations are said to be severe, compared to other academies. You are requested to leave your work for the entrance exams. As a result of internal matters and cuts in expenditure by the State the Rijksacademie plans to concentrate on post-graduate education. Regular exhibitions by students in the exhibition hall.

Ateliers 63, Zijlsingel 6, Haarlem. Telephone 023-321375. Post-graduate education. Entrance exams. (see: Artists workshops).

Some people prefer to have a Teacher's-Education in combination with art-studies.

Lerarenopleiding Vrije Leergangen/Vrije Universiteit, VLVU, Rijnsburgstraat 11, A'dam west. Telephone 178793. Bus 23.

Instituut voor Opleiding van Leraren d'Witte Leli, Nieuwe Spiegelstraat 17, A'dam centrum. Telephone 225496.

Private art-classes

No serious art-schools, operated by private teachers can be recommended for professional art-students. Nevertheless brochures about these courses can be found at the **MAIC. Jan Willem Brouwersplein 9,** A'dam zuid. Telephone 799623. Tram 3, 5, 12, 16 (Van Baerlestraat, Concertgebouw).
They also inform you about non-professional art courses, as organised by:

De Werkschuit, Mauritskade 24, A'dam oost. Telephone 920093. Bus 22; tram 10.
Various art courses.

Nutsatelier, Eerste Weteringsplantsoen 6, A'dam centrum. Telephone 220467. Tram 6, 7, 10 (Weteringschans).

De Moor, Bethaniënstraat 9-13, A'dam centrum. Telephone 224899. Metro Nieuwmarkt.
Video-art, photography courses.

Crea, Grimburgwal 10, A'dam centrum. Telephone 262412. Tram 4, 9, 14, 16, 24, 25 (Muntplein).
Students-cultural organization, also for non-students.

OTHER ART-SCHOOLS

Filmacademie, Overtoom 301, A'dam centrum. Telephone 184352. Tram 1, 6.

Muzieklyceum, Keizersgracht 62, A'dam centrum. Telephone 253054. Tram 13 (Westermarkt), conservatory.

Sweelinck Conservatorium, Bachstraat 5, A'dam zuid. Telephone 730303. Bus 26; tram 24 (Beethovenstraat).
Conservatory.

Theaterschool, Grimburgwal 10 G, A'dam centrum. Telephone 261241. Tram 4, 9, 16, 24, 25 (Muntplein).

GENERAL INFORMATION

Most guides about Amsterdam are written in Dutch. To avoid getting lost in the city the first thing to do, when you are in Amsterdam, is to buy a good street-map or pocket-atlas.
In the list below some interesting guides and magazines about Amsterdam are mentioned.

Specialised guides:

Amsterdam zak-atlas, official pocket-atlas with grid-index (English-French-German-Dutch).

Amsterdam shopping (Dutch), J. van Genst. Shopping guide.

Museum-guide (English) by H. Vogels, Amsterdam museums, published by Bosch & Keuning.

Amsterdam Ongekend (Dutch) by Ben Ten Holter, published by Bert Bakker. Dutch-written about the ins and outs of the metropolis Amsterdam.

The Rough Guide to Amsterdam and Holland, by Dunford and Holland, edited by Routledge and Kegan Paul. English guide on alternative tourism.

On Foot in Surprising Amsterdam, by Tom Vincent, English written guide.

De Boekhandels van Amsterdam, by Clara Hillen, published by Bridges Books. Dutch guide on Amsterdam bookshops, mentioning primarily their specializations.

Cultural/touristic information magazines

Amsterdam This Week, P.O. Box 3901 (free available at AUB Ticketoffice, Leidseplein) English.

Uitkrant (free available at AUB Ticketoffice, Leidseplein and major post and giro-offices) Uitkrant contains large gallery/alternative spaces diary.

Amsterdam Today, P.O. Box 12392; English written magazine, published every fourteen days, available at news-stands in Leidsestraat and P. C. Hooftstraat. Contains shopping-guide, cultural, culinar information. f 4,95.

Agenda, Marnixstraat 156; Dutch written information/advertisement magazine on Amsterdam, specially meant for a young public. Free available every month in the Amsterdam cafés.

The Paper, Lauriersgracht 116. Telephone 260216.
More serious attempt to make a monthly cultural/information magazine, meant for the over 50,000 English-speakers, living in Amsterdam. Available on news-stands at Spui, Leidsestraat and P. C. Hooftstraat. f 2,95.

INFORMATION ABOUT AMSTERDAM

VVV Tourist Information, Stationsplein 10, A'dam centrum. Telephone 266444. Tram/bus/metro: Central Station.
Open Mon-Sat 9-5. Information by telephone on Sundays and after 5: 221016. Hotel-booking service, general tourist information, housed in building opposite Central Station main entrance.
　Other VVV offices: Leidseplein 15, open daily 9-11pm. A'dam centrum. Tram 1, 2, 5, 7, 10; bus 26. Telephone 221016 and Utrechtseweg (high-way), open Mon-Sat 10.30-2 and 2.30-6.30. From October 1st closed.

Accommodation
Hotels: Ask for a special folder at foreign tourist offices or at VVV in Amsterdam, or **Nationaal Hotel Reserveringscentrum.** The Hague (National Hotel Reservation). Telephone 070-202500.

CAMPINGS

Vliegenbos, Meeuwenlaan 138, A'dam noord. Telephone 368855. Bus 32, 36, 39, 38.

Zeeburg, Zuider IJdijk 34A, A'dam east. Telephone 944430. Bus 37; tram 3, 10 (terminal).

Amsterdamse Bos, Kleine Noorddijk 1, Aalsmeer-Bovenkerk. Telephone 020-416868. Regional CN bus 171, 172.

A'damse IJsclub, IJsbaanpad 45, A'dam zuid. Telephone 620916. Tram 6, 16, 24 (walk from terminal); bus 65 (Amstelveenseweg).

Gaaspercamping, Loosdrechtdreef 7, A'dam Gaasperplas. Telephone 967326. Metro Gaasperplas.

YOUTH-HOTELS

Sleep-in, Mauritskade 26, A'dam east. Telephone 947444. Tram 3, 6, 9, 10; bus 58.
Open Easter, Whitsun, summer.

Vondelpark NYHF, Zandpad 5, A'dam zuid. Telephone 831744. Tram 1, 2, 5, 7, 10 (Leidseplein); bus 26.

Other commercial youth and low-budget hotels are mentioned in a special brochure, available at the VVV tourist office.

TRAVEL IN AMSTERDAM

Using public transport in Amsterdam is advisable, even when you arrive by car.
First trams/buses/metro-trains depart at 6.30, the last leave around midnight. At 1.30 night-buses start. The inner-city and the canal-zones are generally jammed during weekdays, so riding on trams or the metro can be less exhausting. The drivers of buses and trams gladly tell you where to get out. The metro-lines in Amsterdam are not yet as extensive as the bus or tramlines, and they generally run above ground. If you spend one day in Amsterdam, using public transport, then buy a ticket for f.8.05, to criss-cross all Amsterdam zones in one day. Also 2, 3 and 4 day tickets are available.
Day-tickets are sold by the drivers, more day-tickets you can buy at the GVB information offices opposite **Central Station (next VVV tourist office),** opened 11. Leidseplein ticket-booth, open 8.30-2.30 and in the hall of the Amstelstation, open 7-8. Information: 272727 (from 7-11).
Next to the day-tickets most passengers buy 'strippenkaarten': **strip-tickets.** Tram and bus-drivers only sell 6-strip tickets and 10-strip tickets. It's less expensive to buy a 15-strip ticket at the above mentioned GVB-offices or at tobacconists or post-offices. Amsterdam has been divided into 11 zones. Tourists will generally travel within the one or two inner-city zones of Centrum and Zuid. Network/zones are shown in every tram/bus shelter. These shelters also mention the 'name' of the stop. What to do when entering tram bus or metro? Stamp — or ask the driver to do so — 2 strips for one zone, 3 for 2 and so on, in the yellow stamping machine next to the entrance in bus or tram or metro-stations. If you 'forget' to stamp, a bunch of courageous — usually not uniformed — inspectors can surprise you asking for your ticket. Fines are f 26,- and without money in your pocket, they can take you to the nearby police-office. Night-buses take off after midnight when regular lines are stopped. A special folder Nightbuses/Nachtbussen is free available at the GVB information-offices. Instead of large advertisements all Amsterdam metro-stations are decorated by monumental art-works. **Metro-station Nieuwmarkt** shows the battle that former inhabitants fought against the police, trying to prevent the demolition of their tumble-down area.

TAXI

The international way to catch a taxi, making gestures to the drivers, never seems to work out in Amsterdam. It is better to phone or walk to the nearest taxi-stand. During peak-hours on rainy or snowy days some patience is required after phoning the central taxi-number 777777, while waiting for one of the 625 cabs. Although signs claim the tip is included taxi-drivers say 'dank-u-beleefd': they like to receive a small financial appreciation.

BIKES

Most Amsterdammers seem to possess a bicycle. Join them, by renting a bike for one day, but only if you are experienced enough to face the heavy traffic in the inner city. In most cases cyclists have to creep through narrow paths between parked vans, honking cars and the tram always keeping an eye on the tram-rails, which have to be squarely crossed in order not to get stuck or skid over them. Also don't forget to lock your bike! Practise in the lush green country-side of Amsterdam. Cyclists can take bikes in the metro.

Bike-hire centres

Fiets-o-fiets, Amstelveenseweg 880-900, A'dam zuid, next to entrance of Amsterdamse Bos. Bus 65.

Rent-a-bike, Stationsplein 6, A'dam centrum, left-side at the front of Central Station.

Koenders, Utrechtsestraat 105, A'dam centrum. Telephone 234657. Tram. 4.

Vulling, Vossiusstraat 1, A'dam zuid. Tram 1, 2, 5, 7, 10 (Leidseplein), next to Vondelpark main-entrance.

TRAVEL OUTSIDE AMSTERDAM

Instead of the organised city-and-surrounding trips by tourists-companies, yellow regional buses take you to the same places for cheaper. These regional buses leave from different places in Amsterdam. You can use your 'strippenkaart' in these buses.

Regional bus-stops/terminals

Prins Hendrikkade, near the St. Nicolaas-church opposite Central Station, NZH buses with direction **Edam, Volendam, Marken, Hoorn, Purmerend and KLM bus direction Schiphol Oost and Schiphol Centrum Airports.**

Amstelstation, CN buses to Schiphol Airports, Amstelveen, Amsterdamse Bos.
For a cheap but long ride to the beaches of **Zandvoort** and **Bloemendaal**: take the NZH bus, leaving from the parking-garage near the Marnixstraat, police-office. At the same spot buses depart for London.

Information about travel in Amsterdam: 272727 (daily from 7-11); and **outside Amsterdam: 245337** (daily from 7-11).

CAR HIRE

Next to international organizations, smaller companies like Kuperus, Budget, KAV, Drive-yourself or Diks offer reasonable rates. Addresses and telephone-numbers, see: van hire, mentioned in the caption Useful art addresses.

TRAINS

The **Central Station** has connections with all major national and European cities. Information: **238383** (8-10).

Amsterdam railway stations are:

Centraal Station, Stationsplein, A'dam centrum. Terminal of tram 1, 2, 4, 9, 13, 16, 17, 24, 25; bus 18, 21, 22, 23, 29, 32, 33, 34, 39, 56, 67 and two metro lines.

Amstelstation, Julianaplein 1, A'dam oost. Tram 12; bus 8, 15, 56; metro-station. Trains and metros with direction south-east of Amsterdam: Utrecht, Nijmegen etc.

Muiderpoortstation, Oosterspoorplein, A'dam oost. Tram 3, 6; bus 8, 22, 36, 38, 59.

Station RAI, Europaboulevard 6, A'dam Buitenveldert. Tram 4; bus 8, 53. Trains to Schiphol Airport.

RAI Station is near the RAI exhibition/conference centre and has no railway-connection with Central Station, so take tram 4.

Sloterdijk, Molenwerf 6, A'dam Sloterdijk. Tram 12, 14; bus 15, 18, 36, 42, 68. Trains direction Haarlem, Zandvoort. This station is near what was once a village with a picturesque church.

Bijlmerstation, Bijlmerdreef, A'dam Bijlmermeer. Bus 50, 51, 53, 126; metro. Trains direction Utrecht.

Zuidstation, Zuidplein, A'dam nieuw zuid. Tram 5; bus 65, 66.
Another new, rather isolated, station. Trains direction Rai Station and Schiphol Airport. Next to Zuidstation the Amsterdam World Trade Center is (being) built. This station is only by tram 5 connected with the Central Station.

TRAVEL ENQUIRIES

Trains from Amsterdam: 238383, Schiphol Amsterdam Airport: 5110432, Schiphol/arrival charters: 5110666, public transport in Amsterdam: 272727, regional transport outside Amsterdam: 245337, taxi: 777777 (six times 7).

Airport

Schiphol Amsterdam Airport is connected with several bus-lines and a train with the inner city, CN buses 143, 144, 145, 173. KLM operates own blue-coloured buses.

TRAVEL ABROAD

If you are under 26 years old Transalpino/BIGE tickets are the cheapest way to travel by train, bus, or plane. Available at Transalpino and NBBS. Some travellers prefer instead of taking the train/boat to London to arrange a more comfortable KLM or British Airways flight, which costs nearly the same. (Late saver prices).

Some travel-companies, offering inexpensive travel.

Amber, Da Costastraat 77, A'dam west. Telephone 851155. Tram 7, 17 (Kinkerstraat).
Cheap travel to non-European countries.

Budget Bus, Rokin 10, A'dam centrum. Telephone 275151. Tram 1, 2, 4, 16, 24, 25.
Cheap return bus fares from Amsterdam, The Hague, Breda, Rotterdam to London and major British cities. Also cheap flights to other destinations.

Iberbus, Vijzelstraat 89, A'dam centrum. Telephone 267068. Tram 16, 24, 25.
Cheapest, but most fatiguing way to travel to Barcelona and other Spanish sun-spots.

KLM, Leidseplein 1, A'dam centrum. Telephone 434242. Tram 7, 10, 12; bus 26.
Cheap flights to London. In England reservations also via British Airways.

Magic Bus, Rokin 38, A'dam centrum. Telephone 264844. Tram 1, 2, 4, 16, 24, 25. Cheap travel by buses, trains, planes to several parts of the world, specially England and America.

NBBS, Dam 17, A'dam centrum. Telephone 237687 or 071-145757. Tram 1, 2, 4, 5, 16, 24, 25.
NBBS, Ceintuurbaan 294, A'dam zuid. Telephone 799337. Tram 16, 24, 25, 3, 12.
Student and youth travel agency. Sells under-26 reduction train/flight tickets all through Europe and some other parts of the world.

Transalpino, Rokin 44, A'dam centrum. Telephone 277454. Tram 1, 2, 4, 5, 16, 24, 25.
Bige-tickets for travellers/students under 26, trains, intercontinental flights, camping-flights. Canada, USA, Latin America, Australia, New Zealand, Europe and Africa. Also city trips to London, Paris, Rome, Berlin etc.

HITCH-HIKING

Lift-centrale, P.O. Box 83-10, Buskenblazerstraat 36 huis, A'dam west. Telephone 846730. Tram 17; bus 15 (Hoofdweg/Postjesweg).
Open daily from 9-5. Membership of this international hitch-hikers service organization costs f 15,- a year, per 500 kilometers you pay f 5,- and take part in sharing the petro-costs. Membership required at least one week before leaving.

CONSULATES

U.S.A., Museumplein 19, A'dam zuid. Telephone 790321, 717030. Tram 2, 3, 5, 12; bus 65, 66, 67, 69 (Johannes Vermeerstraat/van Baerlestraat).

Great Britain, Koningslaan 44, A'dam zuid. Telephone 764343. Trams/bus: see above.

West Germany, De Lairessestraat 172, A'dam zuid. Telephone 736245. Tram 16.

Denmark, De Ruyterkade 139, A'dam centrum. Telephone 234145. Bus 28.

Norway, De Ruyterkade 107, A'dam centrum. Telephone 242331. Bus 28.

Sweden, Koningslaan 39, A'dam zuid. Telephone 644101. Tram 2 (Koninginneweg).

Japan, Keizersgracht 634, A'dam centrum. Telephone 243581. Tram 16, 24, 25 (Vijzelstraat).

Austria, Weteringschans 251, A'dam centrum. Telephone 268033. Tram 6, 7, 10.

Switzerland, Johannes Vermeerstraat 16, A'dam zuid. Telephone 6442231. Tram 2, 3, 5, 12; bus 65, 66, 67 69.

France, Vijzelgracht 2, A'dam centrum. Telephone 225811. Tram 16, 24, 25, next Maison Descartes.

Spain, Jacob Obrechtstraat 51, A'dam zuid. Telephone 796591. Tram 16 (De Lairessestraat).

Italy, Herengracht 609, A'dam centrum. Telephone 240043. Tram 4 (Utrechtsestraat).

Eire, Dr. Kuyperstraat 9, The Hague. Telephone 070-630993.

Canada, Sophialaan 7, The Hague. Telephone 070-614111.

Australia, Koninginnegracht 23, The Hague. Telephone 070-647908.

Belgium, Herengracht 541, A'dam centrum. Telephone 248771. Tram 4 (Utrechtsestraat).

Cultural reduction-passes

Nearly all museums sell a Museumkaart, offering you a whole year's free admittance to over 250 Dutch museums. Without this pass you pay generally about f 5,-. For all young people between 15 and 25 years a similar museum-kaart joins a complete cultural reduction-pass: the **Cultureel Jongeren Paspoort.** It costs only f 9,50, offering in addition to free museum-visits, reductions at the theatre, cinema, concerts and a reduced membership to Public Libraries, Art-hire centres and several cultural magazines. A free monthly magazine is sent to all CJP-members in North-Holland: **Plug.** Cheap travel to Barcelona, Prague, London, Paris and Cologne is organized by Plug in cooperation with SISC Student Travel. The CJP is available at the VVV Tourist office, and the AUB Ticketoffice, Leidseplein.

Bank-opening hours

Bank opening-hours in Amsterdam are: Mon-Fri 9-5, Thursday evening also from 6-7.30, some banks Friday evening 6-7.30. In the Leidsestraat and Rokin special exchange-offices are open during the evening and at weekends. Grenswisselkantoren (GWK) are opened also during weekends, daily from 6.45-10.45. GWK also operates on trains in Europe.

Shopping-hours

Generally, Monday morning and/or afternoon all shops are closed. Otherwise opening hours are: Monday 1-6, Tue-Fri 9-6, Saturdays 9-5. Sundays closed. In shopping-centres some shops re-open on Thursday evening from 7-9. On Sundays and during the evening you have to go to special 'Avondverkoop' shops. Some of these are mentioned in the section 'Food buying'. They are open from 5-11.30. Some books and magazines can also be bought on Sundays at Atheraeum, Nieuwcentrum, Spui, A'dam centrum. Tram 1, 2, 5 (Koningsplein).

Problems section

Only if you are a citizen of an European Community state and have brought the appropriate EEC form with you will medical costs be covered. Otherwise you need travel insurance, as there is no free national health service in Holland. A simple visit to the doctor costs around f 25,-. After normal office hours the Centrale Doktersdienst (Central Doctor's-service) can you tell where to find a doctor on call.

Doctor's service-Centrale Doktersdienst. Telephone (day & night) 791821. Where to find a doctor or dentist

Dental clinic, Louwesweg 1, A'dam Sloten. Telephone 156936, ext. 169. (Johan Huizingalaan). Bus 18.
Dental service, telephone 791821, where to find a dentist.

Pharmacies and drug-stores, open from Mon-Sat 8-6.30. Some have Sunday-service. Information: 948709.

First aid, casualty, hospitals
Medical Help-Eerste Hulp kruispost, Oude Zijds, Voorburgwal 127, A'dam centrum. Telephone 249031. Tram 1, 2, 4, 16, 24, 25 (Muntplein).
Emergencies 5555555 (seven times 5) (day & night).

Onze Lieve Vrouwe Gasthuis OLVG, 1e Oosterparkstraat 179, A'dam oost. Telephone 5999111. Tram 3.

Academisch Medisch Centrum, Meibergdreef 9, A'dam Holendrecht. Telephone 5669111. Metro (Holendrecht).
First aid squad: telephone 5663333.

Police alarm-number: 222222 (six times 2) H.Q. Elandsgracht 117, A'dam west. Telephone 559111. Tram 17, 7, 10.

Fire-brigade (Brandweer) alarm number: 212121.

Health/social service: 161666. Psychiatric/social problems.

Lost property in trams, buses and metro: 5514911.
GVB, Prins Hendrikkade 108-114, A'dam centrum. Bus 22, 32, 33, 34, 35 (Shipping-house).

General Post Office
Nieuwe Zijdsvoorburgwal 182, A'dam centrum. Tram 13, 17 or tram 1, 2, 5, 14, 16, 24, 25 (Dam). Telephone 211515.
Open 8.30-6, Thursday evening also till 8.30, Saturday 9-12, Sundays closed. Long-distance telephone calls, telegrams: Open daily 8.30-6 via rear-entrance on Singel.

Information about telephone-numbers: 008 (free).
Foreign telephone-numbers: 0018 (free).
Telegrams: 009 (free).

Townhall, O. Z. Voorburgwal 197-199, A'dam centrum. Telephone 5529111. Tram 1, 2, 5, 16, 24, 25 (Rokin).

PARKS AND BOTANICAL GARDENS

Amsterdam possesses over ten parks. All of them open early in the morning, from 7 and close at sundown. Rules about walking on the grass are happily not as strict as in Britain or France.

Vondelpark. Tram 2, 3, 5, 12 or 6, 7, 10 (respectively Constantijn Huygensstraat, front entrance and Overtoom or Amstelveenseweg, back and side entrances).
Large landscape park, designed by 19th century garden-architect Zocher and named after the famous contemporary poet of Rembrandt: Joost van den Vondel. The Vondelpark was created to solve the problems of a swamp, which seriously menaced public health in those days. Now the swamp is transformed into a large pool. During summertime pop-concerts are held near this pool. Other activities in the park are jogging, biking, walking dogs. **The Filmmuseum** in the park and the teahouse have very scenic terraces for sunny days. In the fin-de-siècle Filmmuseum you can visit a library, and watch old movies. A restaurant is also housed in the building, open in the evenings.

Sarphatipark, A'dam zuid. Tram 3, 12, 24, 25 and **Oosterpark,** A'dam oost, tram 3 and 6 were designed according to the same principles. Both parks are smaller and serve as the necessary 'green escape' for local people.

Amstelpark, A'dam Buitenveldert. Tram 4 or bus 8 (Europaboulevard). The ten-year old Amstelpark overlooking the river Amstel was originally used as an exhibition-space for the gardening of international agriculturists. Now slowly-thickening trees give the Amstelpark its own unique atmosphere. The park includes — next to rich flower-beds — some monkeys, two seals, chickens and an exhibition-room: The 'Glazen Huis'. Regular amateur art-shows are held here. Every two years sculptors take part in a national open-air show, organized in the park. Next exhibition 1986. After visiting the Amstelpark, leave through the back-entrance, for a walk near the river Amstel. Some years ago a statue of Rembrandt sketching, was placed here. It seems that he actually worked here on one of his trips around the city. Next to Rembrandt a mill overlooks the river, an authentic wind-mill located here only for whirlwind-visit tourists.

Pole object by Fred van der Linde, Amstelpark

Beatrixpark, behind Rai-congress/exhibitioncenter. Tram 4. Small, friendly park, dating from the fifties.

Floriade, metro Gaasperplas, terminal. A very recent park, extended near the newly built blocks of Bijlmermeer and Bullewijk. Park includes the Zeiss-planetarium, mentioned in the Museums section.

Other parks include sometimes a small children-animal farm like **Gijsbreght van Aemstelpark** (A'dam Buitenveldert). Bus 8 (van Nijenrodeweg) or **Rembrandtpark** (A'dam Slotervaart) bus 18 (Postjesweg).

Begraafplaats Zorgvlied, Amsteldijk 273, A'dam zuid. Tram 25 (walk from terminal, direction Amstel-river, but don't cross it). Most Amsterdam citizens find eternal peace in this park the municipal burialgrounds, created by garden-architect Zocher, who also designed the Vondelpark. The first part of the park is inevitably scenic, and reminds one strongly of 19th century ideas about life and death: crushed pillars, weeping angels and knotted fingers of marble, in a beautiful natural setting. The grave in the imposing pseudo-Greek temple near the front entrance belongs to circus-director Oscar Carré, whose theatre overlooks the other side of the Amstel-river. Carré is just one of the famous citizens buried here.

Amsterdamse Bos, Amstelveenseweg, A'dam zuid/Amsterdamseweg, Amstelveen. Bus 65 (Amstelveenseweg, entrance), bus 26 (terminal).
Largest park connecting Amsterdam with Amstelveen. The Amsterdamse Bos, the only park which can be compared seriously with the Paris Bois de Boulogne, was created by unemployed citizens during the Depression Years. It contains large lawns, natural swimming pools in canals and in the Nieuwe Meer-lake. In the straight Bosbaan swimmingcontests and regattas are held. During the Amsterdam Olympic Games in 1928 it served as an Olympic swimming pool. In the Amsterdam part

of the Bos, the west-side across the Bosbaan is an expansive international hockey field. It is the home of the Dutch world hockey champions. Elsewhere there is a horse-riding-school and a small zoo with bisons. In the Amsterdamse Bos tea is served in the Boerderij Meerzicht, next to the Bosmuseum. A museum-tramway connects the Bos with the Haarlemmermeerstration, elsewhere at the Amstelveenseweg. During summertime extra-buses leave from there as well. (Bus 70).

Jac. P. Thijssepark, Amsterdamseweg, Amstelveen. Leaving the Amsterdamse Bos at the western exit in Amstelveen, you'll find another park.
This park, named after the famous Dutch biologist Jac. P. Thijsse, was designed carefully as a landscape-park, presenting all kinds of vegetation in a natural setting. Near the Amsterdamseweg — the Amstelveen part of Amsterdams Amstelveenseweg — the small, exhibition center of Amstelveen: Aemstelle is located. A white bath-house like musuem with local art-shows.

Botanical gardens

Hortus Botanicus, Plantage Middenlaan 2, A'dam oost. Tram 9, 14; bus 51-56.
Open Mon-Fri 9-4, weekends 11-4. The area between this Hortus Botanicus and the Artis Zoo was created in the 18th century. In those days wealthy Amsterdammers built their houses as if they were planters with their own plantation. Some houses in the 'Plantage' area have not changed since then. The Hortus Botanicus, dates back to 1682, older than the neighbouring houses. In the beginning plants were cultivated here for medical use, now they are selected only for their botanical beauty. The Hortus is also a research centre for Amsterdam University.

Hortus Botanicus VU, Van der Boechorststraat 7, A'dam Buitenveldert. Bus 23, 67 CN 173.
Open Mon-Fri 8-4.15. Botanical gardens of Vrije Universiteit (Free University, founded by protestants) Recently grown beds with cacti, orchids, bromelias. A large hospital overlooks the gardens.

MARKETS

The first market in Amsterdam took place in 1304, while the last weekmarket was set up some months ago. All Amsterdam daily or weekly markets start around 10.30 and close around 6. Sometimes interesting bargains can be made at that time. All markets are closed on Sundays.

Albert Cuypstraat, located between Ferdinand Bolstraat, (tram 16, 24, 25) and Van Woustraat, (tram 4 and temporary also tram 3).
Most complete daily market: food, clothing, fabrics. The influence of foreign Amsterdammers can be found in the enormous choice of fresh exotic fish, vegetables, fruit and oriental shops round the market. You'll find traditional Dutch 'green hareng' (Hollandse nieuwe) next to Surinam 'shaved ice' (schaafijs). Saturdays are very crowded on the 'Cuyp'. Between shopping you can have a cup of coffee or tea among the market people in one of the coffee houses, overlooking the market.

Whiting, haddock, mackerel at Albert Cuyp market

Dappermarkt, Tram 3 Wijttenbachstraat.
Is a similar but smaller daily market, in Amsterdam east.

Noordermarkt, located next to Noorderkerk, Prinsengracht. Take tram 13 (Westermarkt).
Jordanese weekly-textiles and fabric market, every Monday morning from 9-1. Also selection of second hand clothing.

Singel, tram 1, 2, 4, 5, 16, 24, 25 (Muntplein).
Daily flower and plant-market behind Munt-tower, the former Mint-building. Large collection, offering more than Tulips from Amsterdam.

Curiosities at flea-market, Waterlooplein

Amstelveld, tram 4 (Utrechtsestraat).
Weekly flower, plant and seed-market, every Monday morning from 9-1.

Waterlooplein, Valckeniersstraat, tram 9, 14 or metro.
Amsterdams only flea-market. Crowded during the tourist season. The Waterlooplein-market is becoming more and more fashionable. Now pastel-coloured tea-sets and clothing from the early sixties are extremely popular and rising in price. Although there are some antiques, the second-hand furniture, clothes, bikes and technical equipment have the upper-hand, as well as some interesting book-stands.

Free-market, every Queensday (30 April), held everywhere in the city, so you can't miss it.

Looiersgracht 88/Elandsgracht 109 Antique-market. Tram 7, 10 (Marnixstraat, police-office).
Although official antique-dealers pass art, when someone mentions that the Looiersgracht Market sells antiques, you can find here — let us say — intriguing old curiosities: phonographs, records, some furniture, tea-sets and lamps.
Open Mon-Thu and Saturday until 5.

Book-market, Oudemanhuispoort, tram 4, 9, 14, 16, 24, 25 (Muntplein).
Next to the Justice Faculty, some old and sometimes really interesting books are sold under the gate, overlooking the Oude Zijds Voorburgwal. Oudemanhuispoort means Gate of the Old Man's Home.

Stamp-market, N. Z. Voorburgwal, tram 1, 2, 5, 13, 17 (Dam or post office).
Every Wednesday and Saturday afternoon philatelists brave the rain, wind and snow in their ingeniously made stands. Also a coins market.

FOOD BUYING

Except for the centre of Amsterdam, big supermarkets can be found in the Jordaan-area or in the side-alleys in the canal-zone, where there are small local shops. Well assorted stores are **Albert Heyn, Vivo,** and **Spar;** cheaper are **Jac Hermans, Dirk van der Broek, Edah, Dagmarkt** and **Aldi-markt.** These supermarkets include a bakery, green-grocer and butcher. Reasonable wine, beer and spirits-shops are **Alberto,** and the **Wijnpakhuis.** Health food addicts can buy **bread** by **Paul Année,** Runstraat 25 (near Prinsengracht) and Bellamystraat 2-4 (A'dam west). **Manna,** Utrechtsestraat and main-branch on Spui is an alternative food-supermarket, including a coffee-shop. Similar shops can be found round the Albert Cuyp-market in Amsterdam south: in Frans Halsstraat. **Remember on Sunday all shops are closed.** Only Jewish Orthodox shops are open, as well as **'Zondagsverkoop'** shops, which are sometimes open in the evening from 6-11.30. Such Sunday opening shops are: Maasstraat 16 (tram 25) and Tweede Sweelinckstraat 5 (tram 13, Wijttenbachstraat).

TEA & LUNCH PLACES

The average Nederlander eats slices of bread at breakfast and at lunch-time, or they visit a lunch-room or snack-bar for a quick snack. Tea is reserved for shopping or after a visit to a museum. The typical Dutch pancake is a treat to enjoy with a cup of tea. Listed below is a selection of reasonably priced places to have lunch, tea or sometimes breakfast. Some restaurants (mentioned in the section on restaurants), also open at lunch-time to serve simple meals, and re-open in the evening.

MUSEUM AREA

Area south of Spui and Muntplein, with southern canal-zone between Leidsegracht and Amstel-river including Museum-quarter.

Rijks, van Gogh and especially Stedelijk offer delicious lunches with soups, snacks, salads and patisserie. Exclusive coffee-shops are located in the streets round Stedelijk and Rijks: P. C. Hoofstraat, Willemsparkweg. Near the Albert Cuyp-market you can enjoy cheaper, more exotic lunches.

The Salad Garden, Weteringschans 75, A'dam centrum. Telephone 234017. Tram 6, 7, 10.
Opposite Rijksmuseum. Mostly vegetarian, non-macro-biotic meals with summer-terrace on the Zieseniskade. Huge salad-bar and astonishing vegetable pies. Prices about f 12,-. Open from 11-9.

Park Avenue, Willemsparkweg 67, A'dam zuid. Telephone 626206. Tram 2.
American and English breakfast.

Betty's Coffeeshop, Rijnstraat 75, A'dam nieuw zuid. Telephone 445896. Tram 25.
Jewish 'kosher' coffee-shop, with 'ginger-boluses', fish-cakes and so on. Also open on Sunday, so closed on Saturdays.

Brasserie van Baerle, Van Baerlestraat 158, A'dam zuid. Telephone 791532. Tram 3, 5, 12.
Ever met hedonists? Well, you'll find them in this brasserie, having a champagne-spread meal.

Taller, Keizersgracht 607, A'dam centrum. Telephone 246734. Tram 16, 24, 25 (Vijzelstraat).
Coffee-shop full of Latin-American artists and theatrical people. Next to Museum Fodor.

Het ronde blauwe theehuis, Vondelpark 5, A'dam centrum. Telephone 626642. Tram 1, 6 (Overtoom).
Tea in a beautiful New Objectivist building this tea-house looks like an Enormous Flying Saucer that has descended onto the Vondelpark. Open during early spring and summer.

Flipper, Eerste van der Helststraat 42, A'dam zuid. Telephone 796689. Tram 16, 24, 25 (Ferdinand Bolstraat).
A snack-bar. Typical Dutch snacks are — next to 'frites' — fricadellen, croquets, meat-balls and various 'nasi' and 'bami' balls/slices.

Back-stage, Utrechtsedwarsstraat 67, A'dam centrum. Telephone 223638. Tram 4 (Utrechtsestraat).
Friendly coffee-shop and boutique, directed by Greg and Gary Christmas, two American-born Indian twins.

Le Soleil, Nieuwe Spiegelstraat 56, A'dam centrum. Telephone 227147. Tram 6, 7, 10 (Weteringschans).
Twenty different types of tea, served in the street opposite the Rijksmuseum — with twelve varieties of pancakes. Also on Sundays.

Manna, Spui 1, A'dam centrum. Telephone 253743. Tram 16, 24, 25 (Rokin).
Vegetarian supermarket with small lunch-room on balcony.

Vroom & Dreesmann, Kalverstraat 201, A'dam centrum. Telephone 220171.
Big store with small lunch/snack counter.

De Bijenkorf/La Ruche, Damrak 90A, A'dam centrum. Telephone 218080. Tram 4, 9, 16, 24 25 (Dam).
Another big store including cheap and good restaurant/lunch-room 'La Ruche' and other small coffee-shops.

Pander/De Bonnetterie, Kalverstraat 183, A'dam centrum. Telephone 262162. Tram 1, 2, 4, 16, 24, 25 (Muntplein).
Lunches, patisserie: rare chic on street-level. According to professional coffee-tasters one of the best espresso bars in Amsterdam.

JORDAAN AREA

Area west of Dam-square and Muntplein, with western canal-zone between Haarlemmerstraat and Leidsegracht including the Jordaan quarter.

De Ontbijtkamer, Gasthuismolensteeg 5, A'dam centrum. Tram 1, 2, 5, 13 (N. Z. Voorburgwal, post-office).
A recently-opened Breakfastroom. Open: Only weekends from 5-2. Prices below f 10,-.

Eetsalon Rosmarijn, Gasthuismolensteeg 9, A'dam centrum. Telephone 264239. Tram: see above.
Example of typical Dutch 'broodjeszaak'. Several types of bread with roast beef, egg, croquet and so on. The salon was decorated during the fifties, a now-popular style with mirrors and tiles. Prices below f 10,-.

Hotelschool de Kogge, Elandsgracht 70, A'dam centrum. Telephone 238428. Tram 7, 10 (Marnixstraat, police-office).
High-quality lunches served by hoteliers-to-be. Low prices, because you are the main object of the lesson.

Tea and cakes, 2e Laurierdwarsstraat 60, A'dam centrum (Jordaan). Tram 13 (Westermarkt).
Cornish pastries, quiches, pies, with agreeable prices. Opposite the English Bookshop.

Bredero, O. Z. Voorburgwal 244, A'dam centrum. Telephone 224961. Tram 1, 4, 16, 24, 25 (Dam).
Pancake-home, also soup and dessert.

Koffiehuis De Hoek, Prinsengracht 341/Reestraat, A'dam centrum. Telephone 264430. Tram 13 (Westermarkt).
No-nonsense, traditional coffee-house. Decent opening-hours, no alcohol.

Old Dutch pancakehouse, Westermarkt, A'dam centrum. Tram 13.
Several varieties of pancakes.

D'Theeboom, Singel 210, A'dam centrum. Tram 13, 14, 17 (Raadhuisstraat).
Lunch, wine-bar in a hi-tech interior. Prices from 25 to 30 guilders.

Munchies, Herenstraat 36, A'dam centrum. Tram 1, 2, 5, 13, 17 (N. Z. Voorburgwal).
Snacks, salads, pies, cakes and a fully English breakfast. Herenstraat connects Heren- with Prinsengracht.

Pompadour, Huidenstraat 12, A'dam centrum. Telephone 239554. Tram 13, 17 (Westermarkt).
Patisserie/konditorei, where you can try the exclusive artistic products on the spot. The patissier was educated as a ceramist, but changed his profession to his choice passion.

Robert et Abraham Kef, Marnixstraat 192, A'dam centrum. Telephone 262210. Tram 10.
Cheese-tasting lunch-room, but only twelve seats available. Closed on Monday.

Witch one this one, 1e Bloemdwarsstraat 1, A'dam centrum (Jordaan). Telephone 235639. Tram 13 (Rozengracht).
Milk-shakes, espresso-coffee, Limburg fruit-flans, juices.

Egg-cream, Sint Jacobstraat 19, A'dam centrum. Telephone 230575. Tram 1, 2, 13 (Nieuwe Zijds Kolk).
Breakfasts, healthy snacks, vegetarian meals.

Bananas, St. Antoniebreestraat 77, A'dam centrum. Telephone 278480. Metro (Nieuwmarkt).
Fresh fruit juices and ice cream in a newly built centre near Rembrandthuis and Waterlooplein-fleamarket.

CAFÉS

The Dutch equivalent of public bars are the cafés — or more affectionately — 'kroeg'. Generally they open round 1 and close at 1, Friday and Saturday evening at 2, cafés with a night-licence close later. The different character of each café is the key attraction. The oldest type; the brown café has smoke-stained or brown-painted walls, while small Persian rugs lie on the table. Lamps and draped curtains complete the atmosphere, as though in a traditional Amsterdam home. Here you are not disturbed by loud background music, for there is sometimes only singing by your joyful fellow-drinkers. Modern cafés are as a reaction painted in white, using glass, steel or zinc as decoration. Some 'eet'-cafés also serve simple meals. Each old city quarter has its own local 'kroeg', but here only some characteristic cafés are mentioned.

AROUND SPUI AND SPUISTRAAT

Karpershoek, Martelaarsgracht 2, A'dam centrum. Telephone 247886. Tram 1, 2, 5, 13, 17.
Possibly the oldest café in Amsterdam. Its history goes back to the 17th century when sailors came here to dance. Enjoy the famous Dutch blond beer, brewed elsewhere in the city or the traditional Dutch winter-pea soup: **snert.**

De Koningshut, Spuistraat 269, A'dam centrum. Telephone 264276. Tram 1, 2, 5.
Traditional, brown café with sand spread out over the floor.

Warstein, Spuistraat 266, A'dam centrum. Telephone 229609. Tram 1, 2, 5.
Modern, decorated bar named after the German beer. Also a restaurant with average prices: good meals, quiches, stews and salads.

Gollem, Raamsteeg 4, A'dam centrum. Telephone 254634. Tram 1, 2, 5 (Spui).
A small café, recommended for beer-fanatics, as nearly 150 beers can be tasted here. Original pilsener-beer from Pilzen in Czechoslovakia great-grandmother of the blond beer, in Holland affectionately known as 'pilsje'. But also browns and stouts from Britain, China, Japan and Belgium.

Hoppe, Spui 18, A'dam centrum. Telephone 237849. Tram 1, 2, 5.
The original worn-out threshold of this British-type bar/saloon has been set next to the new one, for thousands of visitors once used it. Strangely enough most of them prefer to stand outside, looking at the traffic on the Spui. After openings in the near Krikhaar gallery, art lovers move to Hoppe.

AROUND REMBRANDTSPLEIN AND REGULIERSBREESTRAAT

Schiller, Rembrandtsplein 26, A'dam centrum. Telephone 249846. Tram 4.
Traditional brown café-restaurant with nostalgic atmosphere. During the thirties cabaret-artists and painters met in Schiller, directed by an artistical owner Frits Schiller. Some of his paintings decorate the bar. In those days a famous cabaret-artist Pisuisse and his wife were shot down behind the statue of Rembrandt, after visiting Schiller. This legendary 'crime passionel' took place near what is now a skating rink, during winter. In Schiller you can treat yourself to six different hot meals of the day, under twenty guilders each.

Het Hooghoudt Proeflokaal, Reguliersgracht 11, A'dam centrum. Telephone 255030. Tram 4 (Rembrandtsplein).
Bodega, in the two houses De Zon en de Maan (Sun and Moon), where low-priced home-made 'jenever', Holland gin, can be tasted. Also sherry, beer and so on.

Oblomov, Reguliersbreestraat 40, A'dam centrum. Telephone 241074. Tram 4, 9, 16, 24, 25 (Muntplein).
All-white new wave café, designed by young architects Sas/De Vries, who also designed **Walem, Rum Runners** and **36 Op de Schaal van Richter.** In Oblomov people meet, who have nothing in common with the lethargic main-character of Goncharov's moving novel. No, here you'll find over-active trendy artists, television-makers, art-directors. After 10 upstairs a cocktail bar, named Cocktailbar opens. Oblomov serves traditionally Italian pasta for reasonable prices.

Mulder, Weteringschans 163, A'dam centrum. Telephone 237874. Tram 6, 10, 24, 25 (Vijzelstraat).
Nameless cafe, with large terrace where you can watch the Amsterdam working-people hurry to the trams of the Weteringplantsoen. During wintertime nearly all terraces are closed, and so is Mulders.

Het Land van Walem, Keizersgracht 449, A'dam centrum. Telephone 253544. Tram 1, 2, 5 (Leidsestraat).
Another neat, white café, originally designed by Gerrit Rietveld in 1920 as part of the Metz-store. Nowadays only three humble neon-tubes and a steep staircase remind one of the work of the famous architect. Artists and dealers from the nearby galleries eat and drink here.

April, Reguliersdwarsstraat 37, A'dam centrum. Telephone 259572. Tram 4, 9, 14, 16, 24, 25 (Muntplein).
Amsterdam is one of the most important European cities for its 'gay'-scene. This is one of the gay bars in the city, where boys watch the boys go by.
   Other similar bars are **Route 66,** Kerkstraat 66; **Wells Fargo,** N. Z. Voorburgwal 103; **Homolulu,** Kerkstraat 23, **Downtown Coffeeshop,** Reguliersbreestraat 31.

JORDAAN-QUARTER

Officially the Jordaan is the area between Nassaukade and Prinsengracht.

Brandon, Keizersgracht 157, A'dam centrum. Telephone 247806. Tram 13 (Westermarkt).
In no other café will you feel as much at the heart of the city as in Brandon. Here the Wester-tower is reflected in the window. A billiard-room completes the 350 year old café.

De Twee Prinsen, Prinsengracht 127, A'dam centrum. Telephone 249722. Tram 13 (Westermarkt).
Rich variety of bottled or draught beers. Other Prinsen-cafés to visit one after the other are De Prinses and De Prins, numbers 96 and 114 respectively on the Prinsengracht. De Twee Prinsen serves also vegetarian meals, pizza, tosti's.

De Twee Zwaantjes, Prinsengracht 114, A'dam centrum. Telephone 252729. Tram 13 (Westermarkt).
Café — next the Andriesse gallery — where nice sentimental songs about Jordaan, Westertoren and Mokum are performed with accordion or organ-accompaniment. Join in!

De Bak, Prinsengracht 193, A'dam centrum. Telephone 257972. Tram 13 (Westermarkt).
Café/spare-rib house annexe to a small restaurant where delicious onion-soup is served. Decoration with antique train-signs.

Nol, Westerstraat 109, A'dam centrum (Jordaan). Telephone 245380. Tram 13, 14, 17 (Rozengracht).
Traditionally Jordaan café with heavy brass and red plush decoration to make your stay here more comfortable. During the Jordaan-festival in September the Nol is more crowded than ever, with singing visitors, accordion-music; so you can not avoid dancing the polonaise afterwards.

De Bel, Lindengracht 108, A'dam centrum (Jordaan). Telephone 240830. Tram 13, 14, 17 (Rozengracht).
Another typical Jordaan café.

Oerwoud, Haarlemmerdijk 165, A'dam centrum. Telephone 269853. Tram 3 (Haarlemmerplein).
Ever spent an evening in a jungle after watching a film? In Oerwoud you can discuss the film you just watched in The Movies cinema, opposite the café. Regular exhibitions by the artistic visitors. Alcoholic gorillas are not allowed to enter.

Het Nieuwe Paleis, Paleisstraat 16/Singel, A'dam centrum. Telephone 260600. Tram 13 (N. Z. Voorburgwal).
Elegant café with early sixties atmosphere. Light beer from Limburg is served here. Screen-prints by Dutch comics-artist Joost Swarte above the bar. Meeting-place of young clean-shaven artists.

THEATRE-CAFÉS/RESTAURANTS

De Blincker, St. Barbarenstraat 7/Nes, A'dam centrum. Telephone 271938. Tram 4, 16, 24, 25 (Rokin).
Zinc-decorated new-wave theatre café, around the corner of Theater Frascati, Nes 63. Plumbers must feel at ease here!

Bodega Keyzer, Van Baerlestraat 96, A'dam zuid. Telephone 711441. Tram 3, 5, 12, 16.
In Keyzer meet classical music-lovers, after a concert in the near Concertgebouw. Some journalists work in the calm atmosphere, guarded by correct waiters. The restaurant is French-Dutch orientated. Prices from f 35,-. Special treat: sole meunière. Sometimes very crowded, Sundays closed.

Américain, Leidsekade 97, A'dam centrum. Telephone 234813. Tram 1, 2, 6, 7, 10. Near Stadsschouwburg.
Wining and dining in architectural beauty. During many decades Américain was the meeting place of writers and actors. The word went around that a Dutch writer became famous, only by receiving constant telephone-calls here. Indonesian and Dutch restaurant, price about f 30,-

De Smoeshaan, Leidsekade 80, A'dam centrum. Telephone 250368. Tram: see above.
Foyer, café and restaurant to dine before performance elsewhere in this former television-studio Bellevue. Reservations advisable.

Art dèco interior of café restaurant Américain, Leidseplein

Odeon, Singel 460, A'dam centrum. Telephone 249711. Tram 1, 2, 5 (Koningsplein).
Theatre-café, annexe dancing.

De Brakke grond, Nes 45, A'dam centrum. Telephone 240394. Tram 4, 16, 24, 25 (Rokin).
Café of the Flemish Cultural Centre. During the turn of the century the Nes-area was filled with brothels and ooh-la-laaa-theatres. Perhaps its name — the brackish ground — is reminiscent of those days.

De Suikerhof, Prinsengracht 361, A'dam centrum. Telephone 227571. Tram 13, 14, 17 (Westermarkt).
Café with platform, where classical music or cabaret is performed.

TD, Keizersgracht 772, A'dam centrum. Telephone 250023. Tram 4 (Utrechtsestraat).
Theatre-café connected with Indonesian restaurant **Tempo Doeloe,** Utrechtsestraat 75, prices from f 17,-In TD classical music and radio-shows are performed here.

Shaffy, Keizersgracht 324, A'dam centrum. Telephone 262321. Tram 13, 17 (Westermarkt).
Simple café in the theatre where ballet, modern drama and other experimental happenings are presented.

De Balie, Kleine-Gartmanplantsoen 10, A'dam centrum. Telephone 232904. Tram 1, 2, 5, 6, 7, 10 (Leidseplein).
Another similar café in a former town-prison. Signs warn you not to deal in drugs or to gamble for money.

RESTAURANTS

Although Dutch connoisseurs are not very enthusiastic about their own cooking tradition, many Amsterdam restaurants serve very well-prepared traditional Dutch food. Nevertheless the exotic restaurants have the upper hand. **Chinese/Indonesian restaurants** are richly represented. The presence of people from former Dutch colonies of Indonesia, Surinam and the cooking of foreign workers from Italy, Spain, Morocco and Turkey resulted in a wide range of authentic, not too expensive restaurants. Many are in the **Jordaan-quarter** and **De Pijp,** next to the Albert Cuyp-market. Authentic Chinese restaurants you'll find in Amsterdam's tiny **Chinatown between Nieuwmarkt and Binnen Bantammerstraat.** Exclusive and more expensive restaurants are spread around **Leidse- and Rembrandtplein,** where Amsterdam's night-life takes place. Listed is a cross-section of eating-places with minimum prices between f 25,- and f 35,-. A cheaper way to eat is to buy a take-away snack: Italian pizza, Surinam roti-pancake or plain chips in Holland known as 'friet' or patates frites. And don't forget the Lebanese shawarma, a bread-roll, filled with slices of tasty lamb. One important thing to remember when going to Dutch restaurants is the opening-hours. Most Dutch prefer to have their 'hot meal' at 6 on the dot, so restaurants open before 5 and close their kitchens generally at 10. Fortunately there are also some night-restaurants in the city: they include the following list.

MUSEUM-AREA, NEAR LEIDSESTRAAT AND UTRECHTSESTRAAT

Casa di David, Singel 426, A'dam centrum. Telephone 245093. Tram 1, 2, 5 (Koningsplein).
Recommended by Italians living in Amsterdam, Casa di David is set in a Venetian-type house between two canals: Singel and Beulingsloot. Home-made pasta, osso bucco, scallopini. Average prices, but not very inexpensive: Quality counts.

Rose's Cantina, Reguliersdwarsstraat 38, A'dam centrum. Telephone 259797. Tram 4, 16, 24, 25 (Muntplein).
Overcrowded Mexican restaurant to dine in during hot summer nights. One of a range of exotic neighbouring restaurants in the Reguliersdwarsstraat near the Flower Market. If already full follow the street to Oblomov, Camargue and so on.

Djawa, Korte Leidsedwarsstraat 18, A'dam centrum. Telephone 246016. Tram 1, 2, 5 (Leidsestraat).
The Indonesian kitchen can be regarded as a second Dutch speciality, for many Dutch were born or lived during their youth in Indonesia. Djawa is a moderately priced speciality-restaurant. Various menus, including the traditionally **'rijsttafel'** tiffin, including over 20 dishes with beef, pork, chicken, shrimps, eggs etc. Speciality of Djawa is 'oedang flambé', large fried shrimp.

Granada, Leidsekruisstraat 13, A'dam centrum. Telephone 251073. Tram: see above.
Simple Spanish restaurant offering paella and special fish dishes.

Sluizer, Utrechtsestraat 41-45, A'dam centrum. Telephone 263557/ 226376. Tram 4.
Two renowned Dutch restaurants, one presenting straight Dutch winterfood, the other one offering a range of delicate fish-specialities, better known as 'fruit de mer.'

De Oase, Achtergracht 19, A'dam centrum. Telephone 265967. Tram 7, 10 (Frederiksplein/Sarphatistraat).
Lunch and diner, natural food and fish restaurant, Japanese tempura. Take-away service.

Orient Fast Food, Utrechtsestraat 89, A'dam centrum. Telephone 279416. Tram 4.
Daily opened Indian/Pakistani restaurant/take-away centre. Traditional, tasty, oriental food. Low prices.

The Golden Temple, Utrechtsestraat 126, A'dam centrum. Telephone 268560. Tram 4.
Vegetarian restaurant with turban service.

Djanoko, Van Baerlestraat 61, A'dam zuid. Telephone 629665. Tram 3, 5, 12; bus 26.
Another reasonably-priced Indonesian **'rijsttafel'** restaurant, decorated with Balinese 'wajang' (shadow puppet), krisses and masks. Carefully prepared assortment of dishes.

De Knijp, Van Baerlestraat 134, A'dam zuid. Telephone 714248. Tram: see above.
French type bistro/restaurant, visited by musicians playing here or in the near Concertgebouw. Cosy decoration.

Kyo, Jan Luykenstraat 2A, A'dam zuid. Telephone 716916. Tram 3, 5, 12 (Van Baerlestraat).
Suki-yaki, sashimi: Japanese eating with chop sticks, opposite the Rijksmuseum. One of the least expensive in the city.

Le menu, Spiegelstraat 27, A'dam centrum. Telephone 253376. Tram 6, 7, 10 (Weteringschans).
Tasty generous portions of meat, inexpensive dining above Café Hans en Grietje.

Yoichi, Weteringschans 128, A'dam centrum. Telephone 226829. Tram 6, 7, 10 or 4.
Recently re-opened Japanese restaurant located in a 19th century monumental house. Food prepared at your table, while Japanese businessmen swarm around the bar. The manager is dressed in traditional costume, and so are his fellow-workers here.

Baldur, Weteringschans 76, A'dam centrum. Telephone 244672. Tram: see above.
Vegetarian restaurant, Anthroposophical, so the dishes are also attractively presented.

Tempura, Weteringschans 99, A'dam centrum. Tram: see above.
Very simple and therefore cheapest Japanese grill-restaurant. Good food, but it closes early in the evening.

Swart, Willemsparkweg 87, A'dam zuid. Telephone 760700. Tram 2.
Hide-away kosher restaurant with Yiddish specialities: kugel and pears, 'gefillte fisch' and so on. Not inexpensive.

Meschibath Nefesch, De Lairessestraat 13, A'dam zuid. Telephone 767622. Tram 16.
Open from Monday to Wednesday. Unique kosher Jewish/ Dutch menus, preparation of food with rabbical supervision. Prices are

reduced for students (with college-card), generally minimum-price round f 12,-.

Opatya, Hobbemakade 64-65, A'dam zuid. Telephone 719495. Tram 16 (Johannes Vermeerstraat).
First Amsterdam Yugoslavian restaurant, meat-dishes, chee-wap-chee-chee, slicovic (prune-liquor). Average prices. Opatya has more branches in the city.

Mirafiori, Hobbemastraat 2, A'dam zuid. Telephone 623013. Bus 26 or walk from Leidseplein/Vondelpark.
Typical Italian restaurant, although overlooking the Vondelpark and not the Tiber. Dishes with fish and lamb specialities. Minimum menu-prices around f 17,-.

Wildschut, Roelof Hartplein 1, A'dam zuid. Telephone 738622. Tram 3, 5, 12, 16, 24, 25.
Newly opened restaurant with carefully decorated interior Art deco furniture, stained glass windows in typical Amsterdam School style. You can have breakfast, lunch and enjoy simple, fresh plats du jour at reasonable prices. Sometimes a VPRO radio-programme is recorded here so please don't talk too loudly.

Lyceum, Cornelis Krusemanstraat 15, A'dam zuid. Telephone 627532. Tram 16.
Another Amsterdamse School restaurant to have your meal after visiting the architectural highlights in this part of the city. The name of the restaurant is derived from the near Amsterdam Lyceum (secondary grammar-school). Special mussel-dishes, tournedos, Wiener-braten, but also Dutch food served in an open, spacious restaurant-room.

Witteveen, Ceintuurbaan 256, A'dam zuid. Telephone 624611. Tram 3, 12, 24, 25. Jazz on Sundays in Winter.
Straight Dutch traditional café/restaurant with a large billiard-room, decorated as if it was a living-room. Prices around twenty guilders. On the other side of the Ceintuurbaan, in the direction of the Amstelriver, crossing the Ferdinand Bolstraat there are more exotic restaurants: Chinese, Spanish and Yugoslavian.

Djokja, Ferdinand Bolstraat 13, A'dam zuid. Telephone 716269. Tram 16, 24, 25.
Reasonable Indonesian restaurant. Sometimes overcrowded. Famous rijsttafels, large 'tiffins' with several side-dishes.

Artist, Eerste Sweelinkstraat 24, A'dam zuid. Telephone 714264. Tram 3, 12 (Ceintuurbaan).
Peaceful Lebanese restaurant serving many vegetarian dishes. Owners are refugees from Lebanon, one of them is a professional magician. The Eerste Sweelinkstraat is a side alley off Albert Cuypstraat near Sarphatipark.

Van Halen, Saenredamstraat 39 huis, A'dam zuid. Telephone 762495. Tram 16, 24, 25 (F. Bolstraat).
Reasonably priced, modern French/Belgian restaurant. The specialities differ, according to the season. Sometimes a rather special Belgian treat: eel-in-green is served. In this area near the Albert Cuyp-market there are several cheap exotic eating-places. The **Gerard Doustraat,** beside the F. Bolstraat, has many.

Harvest Arts, Govert Flinckstraat 251, A'dam zuid. Telephone 769995. Tram: see above.
Small vegetarian restaurant. Everyone speaks English here, so don't worry. Art on the walls.

De Waaghals, Frans Halsstraat 29, A'dam zuid. Telephone 799609. Tram: see above.
Vegetarian dare-devils (as name indicates) serving low-priced meals.

Datscha Alexander, Rustenburgerstraat 160, A'dam zuid. Telephone 735420. Tram 4 (Van Woustraat).
A unique Russian restaurant which is available only by reservation. Decoration reminds visitors of good old pre-Revolution days, sometimes in an estate, waiting for Turgenev to enter. Expensive menu but recommended.

Gandhi, Ferdinand Bolstraat 137, A'dam zuid. Telephone 763388. Tram 3, 12, 24, 25.
Non-violent halal meat-restaurant. Founded recently, but because of its grill specialities, roti, tandoori and chicken and low prices, Gandhi is already world famous in Amsterdam-south.

AROUND DAM-SQUARE AND ROKIN, WARMOESSTRAAT, O. Z. VOORBURGWAL

Pampa Argentina, Rokin 87, A'dam centrum. Telephone 249199. Tram 4, 9, 14, 16, 24, 25.
Argentinian grill-restaurant with live melancholy or uptempo local music. Minimum menu-prices around f 20,-.

O'Henry, Rokin 89, A'dam centrum. Telephone 251498. Tram: see above.
Typical British pub annexe steak and kidney-pie restaurant, and fish-and-chips for homesick British.

Kopenhagen in 't Kaperschip, Rokin 84, A'dam centrum. Telephone 249376. Tram:
Lunch-place and Danish restaurant, decorated as if you're abroad, sailing to the Kattengat. Classic smørgasbrød, as well as many fish-dishes cod, salmon and sole.

Norway-Inn, Kalverstraat 65, A'dam centrum. Telephone 262326. Tram:
Reasonable Norwegian restaurant, hidden upstairs off the Kalverstraat and Rokin. After soup you may attack the huge buffet-table and eat as much as you like, or have the courage to do, because other guests see their fellow gluttons. Shameless children will enjoy this restaurant, they even have reductions for them.

Turkiye, N. Z. Voorburgwal 169, A'dam centrum. Telephone 229919. Tram 1, 2, 5 (general post office).
Moussaka accompanied by a Turkish band and an attractive belly-dancer.

Dorrius, N. Z. Voorburgwal 336-342, A'dam centrum. Telephone 235875. Tram 1, 2, 5 (Spui).
At last an authentic no-nonsense Dutch speciality restaurant. Dorrius is responsible for the tempting smell of mussels, prepared in front of the

restaurant. Few people can resist this while waiting for the tram on a cold afternoon in the city. Also other Dutch traditional dishes.

Die Port van Cleve, N. Z. Voorburgwal 178-180, A'dam centrum. Telephone 240047. Tram 13, 14 (post-office).
All-Dutch lunch-room/restaurant. A hundred years ago a favourite meeting-place for writers of the Tachtigers-literary movement. Now famous for the winter-dishes and gigantic 'biefstukken' (grilled round steaks) served with boiled potatoes, onions, and carrots. Average menu-prices.

Treasure restaurant, N. Z. Voorburgwal 115, A'dam centrum. Telephone 234061. Tram 1, 2, 5, 13, 17.
During the Thirties many Chinese came to Amsterdam and started in business as 'peanut-sellers', most of them have now turned to the restaurant business. One of these authentic-based restaurants is the unspoilt Treasure. Special classic Chinese/Cantonese cooking: Crusty vegetables, peking-duck, pork, red-beans-pie, hidden eggs and so on.

JORDAAN AREA, FROM CENTRAL STATION TO NASSAUKADE

De Keuken van 1870, Spuistraat 4, A'dam centrum. Telephone 248965. Tram 1, 2, 5, 13, 17 (Martelaarsgracht).
The cheapest eating-place in town. Minimum menu-price is under f 10,-. A communal kitchen with strict Dutch tradition, open at 12 o'clock midday and closed after 7. Closed weekends. Good and a large variety of Dutch dishes; **Hutspot:** carrots, onions and bacon, mashed together. **Snert:** pea-soup, a thick green pea-soup; **stamp-pot:** a mixture of mashed potatoes, vegetables with beef or **kale** with a smoke sausage from Gelderland. You'll enjoy Dutch winterfood especially on severe winter days.

Eucalipto, Haarlemmerdijk 40-42, A'dam centrum. Telephone 230794; bus 22 or tram 3 (Haarlemmerplein).
Portuguese home-cooking: stick-fish and other varieties.

Sultan Ahmet, Haarlemmerdijk 176-178, A'dam centrum. Telephone 248358. Bus/tram: see above.
Turkish delights. Reasonably priced, and belly-dancing — by professional — included.

Moeders Pot, Vinkenstraat 119, A'dam centrum (Jordaan). Telephone 237643. Tram 13, 14, 17 (Rozengracht).
Dutch low-priced one-man restaurant, although the name suggests that Mother cooks here. Placed in hideaway Jordaan street.

't Windekind, Haarlemmerdijk 69, A'dam centrum. Telephone 268755. Bus 22.
One of many vegetarian restaurants with natural macrobiotic food.

Cartouche, Anjeliersstraat 177, A'dam centrum (Jordaan). Telephone 227438. Tram 13 (Westermarkt).
Next to the Grafisch Atelier, the graphic workshop, but not many artists can afford a daily, delicious meal here. A bistro with authentic French touch.

Claes Claesz, Egelantiersstraat 24-26, A'dam centrum (Jordaan). Telephone 255306. Tram 13 (Westermarkt).
Another French exquisite restaurant.

Hartedief, Hartenstraat 24, A'dam centrum. Telephone 258500. Tram 13 (Westermarkt or walk from Dam).
French moderate priced bistro. Fish-dishes and delicious 'steaks'. Listening to Edith Piaf, your fellow eaters on Thursday are shop-keepers, shortly before re-opening their shop.

Waroeng Annie, Hartenstraat 29, A'dam centrum. Telephone 236772. Tram 23 (Westermarkt or walk from Dam).
Cheap Surinam rotie (chicken/pork pancake with hot sauce) restaurant. Another speciality from Surinam is rice with **'garter'** (kouseband, a tall string-bean variety).

Van Puffelen, Prinsengracht 377, A'dam centrum. Telephone 246270. Tram 7, 10 (Marnixstraat/Elandsgracht).
Simple café with authentic French cook in the kitchen. If you order 'caille' don't be surprised to find a humble-looking bird. It tastes very delicious, they say.

De Bast, Huidenstraat 19, A'dam centrum. Telephone 248087. Tram: see above.
Simple vegetarian/macro biotic eating-place.

H'88, Herengracht 88, A'dam centrum. Telephone 244446. Tram 13 (Westermarkt).
Inexpensive, student-restaurant. Dutch food, also cheap accommodation in summertime.

De Griek, Prinsengracht 411, A'dam centrum. Telephone 221314. Tram 7, 10 (Marnixstraat, police-office).
Salads, lamb, beef, prepared according to simple Greek tradition. Don't forget the dolmades.

Other locations in Amsterdam

La rive, Amstelhotel, Prof. Tulpplein 1, A'dam centrum. Telephone 226060. Tram 3, 6, 7, 10.
Located on one of the most beautiful spots in Amsterdam: overlooking the ever-flowing river Amstel. La rive, is an example of haute cuisine in Amsterdam, so impossible not to mention it. Specialities: Huitres de Zélande, (oysters) Suprême de Canard aux échalottes (duck with small onions). Eating in a multi-star awarded restaurant is not cheap, but less expensive than to be a hotel-guest in the beautiful Amstel Hotel.

Rishi Roti Room, 1e Oosterparkstraat 91, A'dam oost. Telephone 928628. Tram 3, 6.
For the necessary contrast with the previous restaurant. Rishi is very inexpensive. Hindi meals, near the Oosterpark.

Tisfris, St. Anthoniebreestraat 142, A'dam centrum. Telephone 220472. Metro (Nieuwmarkt).
Modern café, serving tostadas, plat-du-jours, snacks, vegetarian meals and richly assorted salad-bar.

De Cocosnoot, Elisabeth Wolffstraat 94, A'dam west. Telephone 163494. Tram 13.
5 year old restaurant in Amsterdam west. Surinam, Hindi, Indian meats, soups, pum, rice, roti.

Mirasa, Vespuccistraat 42, A'dam west. Telephone 122196. Tram 7, 13 (Jan Evertsenstraat).
In the sixties many Indonesian people came to live in Holland, when the political situation in the just independent Indonesia changed. Most of them live in the western parts of Amsterdam, Mirasa is one of the many Indonesian restaurants that the Indonesians themselves eat at. The cookery of Mirasa is based on the unique West-Java Djakartan tradition, with **'saté'** and **tahoe** specialities — a pleasant calm atmosphere.

Slotania, Slotermeerlaan 133, A'dam Slotermeer. Telephone 134568. Tram 13.
A rather dull, but nevertheless typical restaurant with nostalgic atmosphere of the early sixties, only to be discovered by melancholic thirtiers.

ALL-NIGHT-RESTAURANTS

Bojo, Lange Leidsedwartsstraat 51, A'dam centrum. Telephone 227434. Night-bus Leidseplein.
Chinese/Indonesian. Open from 6-6.

La Papillon, Stadhouderskade 61, A'dam zuid. Telephone 641323. Night-bus F. Bolstraat/Stadhouderskade.
French. Open 5-4.

Kiekeboe, Vondelpark 3, A'dam centrum. Telephone 123021. Night-bus Leidseplein/Overtoom.
French-Dutch. Located in Flimmuseum. Open 5-4.

FESTIVALS

Holland Festival
Around the first of June the international, highly esteemed Holland Festival takes place in Amsterdam, Rotterdam and The Hague. This official festival, with both traditional and avant-garde theatre, music, ballet, and other dance-groups from Europe, America and non-western countries, lasts till the middle of July. Information about locations in the large Amsterdam theatres is available at Amsterdams Uitburo, Leidseplein/Marnixstraat, telephone 229011 or the secretariate of the Holland Festival, Paulus Potterstraat 12, telephone 623320. Uitburo and VVV Tourist Office inform you also about the Festivals outside Amsterdam.

Summer Festival
Sometimes an alternative theatre-festival is organized by smaller 'marge-theaters' in the city. This Summer Festival, mostly with foreign theatre and dance companies, takes place simultaneously with the official Holland Festival. Artists also perform on the streets. Information: 262321 or 241777.

JAZZ

North Sea Jazz Festival
Halfway through July this 3-day festival takes place in the Congrescentrum of The Hague. VVV Tourist-office in Amsterdam can inform you about it. Other **irregular jazz-festivals** are organized in **August and September** in Amsterdam in De Meervaart Theater. Ask Amsterdam Uitburo Ticket-office, Leidseplein, 249011. Old-style Jazz every September in Breda.

POP-FESTIVALS

The tradition of open air pop-festivals seem to have come to an end. Only Vondelpark organizes simple pop-concerts during the summer in its open-air theatre. At the main-entrance you'll find the programme. In autumn, halfway through September the avant-garde pop-festival **'Pandora Music Box Festival'** is organized in **Rotterdam.**

CLASSICAL MUSIC

During the summer-season **Concertgebouw** organizes special popular summer-evening concerts. A special **Medieval/Old Classical Music Festival,** the **Festival Oude Muziek** is held every last week of August and the following weeks in September in Muziekcentrum Vredenburg and other locations in Utrecht.

Last weekend of August all Amsterdam theatre-companies, theatres, concert halls join in an **'Uitmarkt-festival',** where they present their new programmes on several spots between Dam and Munt-square. This cultural happening is organized by the AUB, Amsterdam Uitburo.

THEATRES

Listed are the theatres, presenting concerts or drama, unrestricted by language problems. During summer-time special sessions for foreigners are held in the **Stadsschouwburg.** Tickets generally are available at the AUB Ticket-office, located in the Stadsschouwburg, Liedseplein/Marnixstraat. Telephone 229011. Tram 1, 2, 5, 7, 10; bus 26, 65, 66, 67. Here you also find the free available 'Uitkrant' and 'Amsterdam this week' with cultural information.

Art theatre, Kerkstraat 4, A'dam centrum. Telephone 259495. Tram 1, 2, 5 (Leidsestraat).
American Repertory Theatre. English speaking.

Carré, Amstel 115-125, A'dam centrum. Telephone 225225. Metro (Weesperplein); tram 3, 6, 7, 10 (Sarphatistraat).
Former circus building. Now musicals, ballets, pop and modern classical concerts are performed here.

Mickery, Rozengracht 117, A'dam centrum. Telephone 244132. Tram 13, 14, 17.
International avant-garde theatre.

Shaffy theater, Keizersgracht 324, A'dam centrum. Telephone 231311. Tram 13, 17 (Rozengracht).
Filmhouse, experimental ballet, drama performances. In the 19th century Grieg, Schumann, and Brahms played here.

Stadsschouwburg, Leidseplein 26, A'dam centrum. Telephone 242311. Tram 1, 2, 5, 7, 10; bus 26, 65, 66, 67.
Municipal theatre. During summertime special programmes for non-Netherlandish speaking visitors.

Stopera, Waterlooplein, A'dam centrum. Tram 9, 14; metro (Waterlooplein).
Townhall and municipal ballet and opera-building replacing these sessions from Stadsschouwburg. **The Stopera will be opened Spring 1986.**

Cinemas/filmhouses

Commercial cinemas (bioscopen) publish their programmes every Wednesday evening and Thursday morning in the newspapers. The same yellow paged information is spread all over windows and shops and restaurants in the city. Sessions are generally at 4, 7.30, 9.30, during weekends also at 1.30 and at midnight. In Holland all films are shown in original version with Dutch sub-titles. Most cinemas are around Leidseplein and Munt Square.

Listed here are the filmhouses, offering art-films, festivals, retrospectives with daily sessions.

A programme of all filmhouses is published in the monthly **Uitkrant.**
Entrance fees are generally lower than in the commercial 'bioscopen'. See also foreign cultural centres.

Amsterdams Filmhous Rialto-Rivoli, Ceintuurbaan 338, A'dam zuid. Telephone 623488. Tram 3, 12, 24, 25.

Filmmuseum/Cinematheek, Vondelpark 3, A'dam centrum/zuid. Telephone 831646. Tram 2, 3, 5, 12 (Constantijn Huygensstraat, front entrance of the park).
Historic or oriental films, but also sometimes retrospective with Hollywood heroes with W. C. Fields, Laurel & Hardy and Chaplin.

Shaffy Filmhuis, Keizersgracht 324 IV, A'dam centrum. Telephone 231311. Tram 13, 17 (Rozengracht).

Kriterion-Studio K, Roetersstraat 170, A'dam oost. Telephone 231708. Tram 6, 7, 10, 14 (Sarphatistraat); metro (Weesperplein).
Also commercial cinema.

MUSIC PLACES

CLASSICAL MUSIC

Bachzaal, Bachstraat 5, A'dam zuid. Telephone 730303. Tram 24; bus 26 (Beethovenstraat).
Classical music by Conservatory-students (and their teachers). Free lunch-concerts.

Het Pand Brandaan, Vinkenstraat 29-31, A'dam centrum. Telephone 220998/226581. Tram/bus/metro: walk from Central Station, direction Haarlemmerstraat/Brouwersgracht.
Medieval and Indian music played by Studio Laren, and guests.

Concertgebouw, Van Baerlestraat 98, A'dam zuid. Telephone 718345. Tram 2, 3, 5, 12.
Amsterdams Concertbuilding with the world-famous Concert-gebouworkest, also during his directorship of the Royal Opera House at Covent Garden — conducted by Bernard Haitink. Free lunch-concerts on Wednesday at 0.30.

Mozes en Aäronkek, Waterlooplein 57, A'dam centrum. Telephone 221305. Tram 9, 14; metro.
Monthly concerts of Indian classical raga-music and dance.

De IJsbreker, Weesperzijde 23, A'dam centrum. Telephone 681805. Tram 3, 6, 7, 10 (Sarphatistraat).
Contemporary classical and avant-garde music.

JAZZ

Information about Jazz events, phone Jazz lijn (Dutch-spoken) 267764.

Bim-huis, Oude Schans 73, A'dam centrum. Telephone 233374. Bus 22, 32, 33, 34 (Prins Hendrikkade, Montelbaans-tower).
Home of the improvisation-jazz musicians.

MUSIC-CAFÉS

De Kroeg, Lijnbaansgracht 163, A'dam centrum (Jordaan). Telephone 250177; tram 7, 10 (Marnixstraat, police-office).
Jazz-sessions, salsa.

Joseph Lamm Jazzclub, Laagte Kadijk 160, A'dam centrum. Telephone 228086. Bus 22 (Kadijksplein, Scheepvaartmuseum).
Old style jazz.

Maloe-Melo, Lijnbaansgracht 160, A'dam centrum (Jordaan). Telephone 253300. Tram 7, 10 (Marnixstraat, police-office). Everyday — except Sunday — this café plays mainly the Blues.

Cab Kaye's pianobar, Beulingstraat 9, A'dam centrum. Telephone 235594. Tram 1, 2, 5 (Koningsplein/Singel).
Closed Sunday and Monday.

Bohemian-Jazz café, Kromboomssloot 14, A'dam centrum. Telephone 241019. Metro (Nieuwmarkt).

Rum Runners, Prinsengracht 277, A'dam centrum. Telephone 274079. Tram 13 (Westermarkt).
Restaurant next to the Westerkerk, with Latin and Tango music.

Antilliaans kollektief, Marcusstraat 18, A'dam east. Telephone 681333. Tram 12; bus 8, 15 (Amstelstation); metro (Amstelstation) Caribbean salsa and latin in a side-street off the Weesperzijde, overlooking the Amstel river.

POP/ROCK

Ask for the weekly **Pop-diary (Uitlijst)** at Uitburo, Leidseplein.

Akhnaton, N. Z. Kolk 25, A'dam centrum. Telephone 243396. Tram 1, 2 (N. Z. Voorburgwal).

Mazzo, Rozengracht 114, A'dam centrum (Jordaan). Telephone 267500. Tram 13, 14, 17.
Audio-visual club, live avant-garde pop/reggae music, dancing, slapsticks, giant tv-screen, video-games.

De Meervaart, Osdorpplein 67, A'dam Osdorp. Telephone 107393.
Tram 1.
Incidental pop, jazz, tango concerts.

De Melkweg, Lijnbaansgracht 234A, A'dam centrum. Telephone 241777. Tram 1, 2, 5, 7, 10; bus 26 (Leidseplein).
Multi-media centre, theatre, pop-music, tea-room, better known as 'Milky Way' by young American and German tourists who look for the 'Magic Amsterdam' of the late sixties. De Melkweg includes a pastel-coloured coffee and tea-house, annexe book-shop, both overlooking the Marnixstraat at the back-side of the theatre (a former milk factory).

Oktopus, Keizersgracht 138, A'dam centrum. Telephone 238195. Tram 13, 14, 17 (Rozengracht).
Filmhouse, pop-music, theatre.

Paradiso, Weteringschans 6-8, A'dam centrum. Telephone 264521. Tram 6, 7, 10.
Former Church-building, now a black-painted theatre with one swinging cross on the roof. Live pop, rock, tango, blues, reggae-centre. To be admitted you must become a member.

FOLK-MUSIC

Folk Fairport, Prinsengracht 282, A'dam centrum. Telephone 225487. Tram 13, 14, 17 (Westermarkt).

Face of Folk, Herengracht 90, A'dam centrum. Telephone 278590. Tram 1, 2, 5 (N. Z. Voorburgwal).

DISCOS

Most dancings and discos are located **around Leidseplein.** Admission only on membership. Discos mentioned are an outline of dancing Amsterdam.

The Danspaleis (Dancepalace) temporary placed during hot summer nights near the Museumstraat

Dansen bij Jansen, Handboogstraat 11, A'dam centrum. Telephone 228822. Tram 1, 2, 5 (Leidsestraat).
Friendly student-disco, (Jansen is a popular surname in Holland.)

DOK, Singel 460, A'dam centrum. Telephone 237503. Tram 1, 2, 5 (Koningsplein).
Disco in cellar of Odeon Theatre. Gay disco, hit-chart music.

Fizz, N. Z. Voorburgwal 165A, A'dam centrum. Tram 1, 2, 5.
Modern avant-garde pop-club, dancing. Fashionable, mixed public. Also large dining-area to watch the dancing crowd. Fizz is in constant rivalry with Mazzo to become the hottest spot in town.

't Nijlpaardenhuis, Warmoesstraat 170, A'dam centrum. Tram 1, 2, 5, 13, 16, 24, 25 (Dam).
Amsterdam's first and only roller-skate dancing.

Zorba the Buddha, O. Z. Voorburgwal 216, A'dam centrum. Telephone 259642. Metro (Nieuwmarkt).
Baghwan-ideology-based disco, but not only visited by red-dressed sanyasins. Visit during weekdays. At the weekends primarily teenagers (anything but the Sirtaki) in Zorba's.

Mazzo, Rozengracht, 114, A'dam centrum (Jordaan). Telephone 267500. Tram 13, 14, 17.
Disco in the grand manner, rock 'n roll, new wave, soul and audio-visual happenings.

Sfinx, Kerkstraat 50, A'dam centrum. Tram 1, 2, 5 (Leidsestraat).
Disco of the beautiful, constantly sun-tanned people.

Flora Palace, Amstelstraat 24, A'dam centrum. Telephone 230469. Tram 9, 14.
Funky and soul music from the charts. Mostly teenage public. Former Disney-cinema.

't Okshoofd, Herengracht 114, A'dam centrum. Tram 13, 14, 17 (Westermarkt).
Simple night-club, disco, videotheque, student visitors.

36 Op de schaal van Richter, Reguliersdwarsstraat 36, A'dam centrum. Telephone 261573. Tram 1, 2, 4, 16, 24, 25 (Muntplein).
Another all-white designed interior. 36 on the Richter-scale, equivalent for a nearly atomic earthquake. Here you can await the first-aid squads, dancing your problems away, reflected in cracked mirrors, while Latin salsa music fills your head.

More traditional night-clubs are around the Rembrandtsplein and Thorbeckeplein.

RECREATION/SPORTS

Information about sports facilities and sports clubs is given by the VVV Tourist-office. Newspaper **Het Parool** sells a map with all Amsterdam sports-fields in its office at the corner of Spui and Rokin.

PUBLIC SWIMMING POOLS (INDOOR)

Heiligeweg, Heiligeweg 19, A'dam centrum. Telephone 236935. Tram 1, 2, 5 (Koningsplein).

Zuiderbad, Hobbemastraat 26, A'dam zuid. Telephone 792217. Bus 26 (Museumstraat).

De Mirandabad, De Mirandalaan 7, A'dam zuid. Telephone 429090. In summer the outdoor swimming-pool is open.

OUTDOOR

Sloterparkbad, Slotermeerlaan 2, A'dam Slotermeer. Tram 13 (terminal).

FREE-NATURE SWIMMING

Nieuwe Meer, Amsterdamse Bos. Bus 65 (Amstelveenseweg) 23 (van der Boechorststraat).

ROLLER-SKATING

Sarphatistraat 67, A'dam oost. Telephone 225488. Tram 10.

CYCLING/BIKE-HIRE

(See: Transport).

CANAL BIKING

Canal-bike, Amstel 57, A'dam centrum. Telephone 265574.
Stations opposite Rijksmuseum, Stadhouderskade. Tram 16, 24, 25.
   Prinsengracht next to Westerkerk, tram 13.
   Keizersgracht near Leidsestraat, tram 1, 2, 5.

Roëll, Mauritskade 1, A'dam oost, behind Amstelhotel, Sarphatistraat. Tram 10.

FOOTBALL-STADIUMS

Ajax and FC Amsterdam are the most important Amsterdam football clubs. Football season is from August until April. Every August an international Amsterdam 700 tournament is held in the Olympic Stadium. For several years now the national football-star Johan Cruyff has not played in his original Ajax-club, so you won't find him in the **Ajax Stadion,** Middenweg, A'dam oost. Tram 9 (terminal) or Olympic Stadium/F.C. Amsterdam, Stadionplein, A'dam zuid. Tram 6, 16, 24 (respective terminals). In the Olympic Stadium also moto-cross and cycle championships are held (August/September).

ATHLETICS

Sportpark, Olympiaplein 20, A'dam zuid. Tram 24; bus 26.

SKATING

Jaap Eden-baan, Radioweg, A'dam oost. Tram 9 (Middenweg); bus 8 (Kruislaan).

INDOOR-SPORTS

Oude RAI Sporthal, Ferdinand Bolstraat, A'dam zuid. Tram 25.

Sporthal Zuid, IJsbaanpad 19, A'dam zuid. Tram 16, 24, 25 (walk from terminal); bus 65 (Amstelveenseweg) near the camping.

BOWLING

Knijn, Scheldeplein 3, A'dam zuid. Telephone 642211. Bus 15.

TENNIS/SQUASH

Tenniscourts: Karel Lotsylaan, A'dam zuid. Bus 26 (Buitenveldertselaan), Sloterplas, Slotermeerlaan, A'dam Slotermeer. Tram 13 (terminal).

Frans Otten-stadion Squash/Tennis, Stadionstraat 10, A'dam zuid. Tram 6, 16 (terminal).

MISCELLANEOUS SPORTS

Formula 1 motor-sports, every last week of August: Grand Prix of Holland, Circuit van Zandvoort (trains from Central Station Amsterdam) Zandvoort, National championship starts around Easter.

Table-tennis: Tafeltenniscentrum, Keizersgracht 209, A'dam centrum. Telephone 245780. Tram 13 (Westermarkt).

Chess-playing/Go: Schaakcafé Het Hok, Lange Leidsedwarsstraat 134, A'dam centrum. Telephone 243133. Tram 1, 2, 5 (Leidsestraat).

Billiards and darts can be played in cafés with indication 'café-billiard' painted on the window. In Holland only continental billiards are played — not snooker.

photo by A. W. Peetoom

Christian Reinewald was born in 1955 in Amsterdam, where he was brought up and studied at the Spinoza Lyceum. He has a diploma in painting and graphic arts from the Gerrit Rietveld Academie. He started writing about culture and art as a freelance journalist and photographer for the monthly magazine Plug. Some of his articles and photos have been published by BBK-krant, Vrij Nederland, Museumjournaal and recently by the Amsterdam newspaper Het Parool and Arts Review, London. He also cooperated in writing a catalogue of the Aorta/Beelstroom exhibition. Between 1982 and 1984 he took part in exhibitions in Amsterdam, Bussum and Den Bosch; two were organized by Museum Fodor and Aorta. The latter artist-space also presented his first solo-exhibition of collages and assemblages, June 1984. At present he tries to combine his journalistic work with his activities as a visual artist.

If you have any suggestions, remarks or new addresses or details to add to this guidebook I would be grateful if you could send them on the sheet printed below.

Christian Reinewald
c/o Amsterdam Art Guide
Art Guide Publications
28 Colville Road
London W11 2BS
England

Name of organisation/gallery/restaurant/bookshop/magazine, etc.

....

....

Address..

....

....

....

Other information ....

....

....

....

....

....

....

....

Thank you.